MELANIE MULAMBA

Loosed

Clovercroft Publishing

Loosed

©2019 by Melanie Mulamba

Published by Clovercroft Publishing, Franklin, Tennessee

Copy Edit by Lapiz Digital Services

Cover Design by Suzanne Lawing

Interior Design by Symbiosys Technologies

Printed in the United States of America

978-1-948484-56-5

Dedication
ᘓ

Every physical, mental, or spiritual distress I have gone through in my journey has purposed me for this moment as I am writing to give hope to women out there. I dedicate this book to those trapped in abusive matrimonial relationships.

I also dedicate it to my parents and siblings for always being there for me, to all my brilliant children for their support and understanding, and, last but not least, to my loving and supportive husband who encouraged me to write this book.

To the many selfless and kind souls placed on my path, I say thank you for your unconditional love.

Preface

CS

Sometimes I wonder if God hears me.
Sometimes I wonder if I could have done better with my life.
Sometimes I wonder if the pain will ever go away.
Sometimes I wonder how life can be so full of surprises.

My name is Celine, and those were my thoughts back in 2000. I was at a breaking point. What little stable ground I had underneath my feet was collapsing. But with God's grace, my own determination, and the help of family and friends along the way, I managed to make it through.

This book is a story about my life. Though the story reveals the terrible and sometimes horrific abuse I faced, it's not a tragedy. It's a message about grace and redemption, and hopefully an inspiration to you.

Although my testimony focuses on abuse, it doesn't matter what your particular obstacle is; this book was still written for you. Right now, you may be struggling with finances, relationships, health, self-esteem, or even death. But you can get through it, be healed, and have peace.

So, what will your story be? After all, tomorrow is another page that has yet to be written. Starting now, take every opportunity to write the pages of your life in a way that will not cause you shame or regret.

Keep in mind that your "Book of Life" is not meant for you. Your book is what you leave for others to be emboldened by, so don't be afraid to be the hero of your own fairytale.

God bless you as you journey forth.

Truly,
Celine

Chapter 1

The little girl knew her mother had snapped and was going to kill her. Before the girl could run away, the mother pounced and took her to the ground with the crazed intent of choking the life out of her. However, it wasn't the rigid and determined fingers gripped around the child's neck that terrified her so. It was her mother's eyes.

It would've been less dreadful if those eyes were at least filled with sickening hatred; that meant some sort of humanity —as vile as it would've been—was still there. Instead, the girl saw animal eyes that were wide and fixed on her. Her mother was gone, far gone, devoid of any spirit except one: the devil.

That little girl was now an adult on a TV show recounting the abuse she endured from her mother. I was riveted by the woman's story, which she told with eerie calm. The more she spoke, the more my body tensed up as memories rippled into my consciousness. I, too, had seen eyes like that glaring down at me as another devil tried to snuff out my life. It wasn't supposed to be that way, though.

I thought back to my childhood and how the manner in which I grew up should've insulated me from that sort of madness. I was a proud child and had every reason to be. I was born in the beautiful town of Lubumbashi to strict yet loving parents, the third of their seven children together. My appearance made me stand out. I was so light skinned that they called me *mundele net a rater*, which means "almost white."

I considered myself to be a daddy's girl. Daddy was an extraordinary man. He went from being a nurse to owning pharmacies to opening his own pharmaceutical factory that still operates to this day. His success gave us access to a chauffeur, gardener, and guards who provided constant security. But we weren't spoiled. Daddy knew the importance of hard work and instilled that value in his children.

Mother was a spiritual warrior who fought battles on her knees. She was the centerpiece of the family, doing her best to make sure the hearth ran properly. Even though Mother was graceful and refined, she was also tenacious when it came to protecting the sanctity of her family.

Although Daddy could easily afford a home in a high-end community, he decided to build our family mansion—more of a compound—in a less desirable neighborhood in Kinshasa. We had ironclad curfews for our protection and rarely had permission to leave the interior confines of the compound. These rules were enforced to prevent us from mingling with unsavory characters that lurked about.

Considering this, Daddy's choice of the neighborhood seemed odd, but it was influenced by his core values. He was a humble man who never let his considerable wealth consume his humility. However, though Daddy's commitment to stay grounded dictated the home's location, he spared no expense in making it paradisiacal for his family.

The façade resembled a fortress and came complete with a double gate and a ten-foot brick wall that surrounded the property. The house itself was nestled at the end of a downward-sloped and curved driveway, obscured from the prying eyes of the public. However, a sumptuous balcony allowed us all-access views of not only our city, but also the capital of the neighboring country.

Interiorly, the home was a work of art. Its expansive layout was lavishly enhanced with copper and marble accents that were brought to life by an Italian architect.

A constant influx of family members filled the house with lively banter and cheer. Not only was our house a hub for blood relatives, but it also was a haven for friends who were considered family. Peter, for example, was friends with my older brother and sisters. He was a gifted musician who played piano at church. Peter's family was so close to ours that Daddy actually helped deliver Peter when he was born.

However, all was not well. I had an intriguing mix of precociousness and innocence that enabled me to be acutely aware of the subtle emotional energetics around me. I uneasily picked up on tension emanating from Mother. This was due to Daddy having children outside of their marriage.

I could feel Mother's pain and humiliation as she continued being a dutiful and faithful wife. My youthful mind had difficulty processing her actions. I just couldn't understand why she was so passive. Sometimes I would just study her as I tried to make sense of it all. She was obviously a beautiful and intelligent woman as well as a dedicated wife and mother: all assets. Moreover, she appeared to have the ability to rebuke the situation and stand on her own if she had to. What made her tolerate the betrayal?

My naiveté afforded me ignorance. It was a veil that shrouded my eyes to Mother's true form—a woman molded by a paternalistic tribal culture that threatened the removal of her children if she didn't comply with the wishes and deeds of her husband. Moreover, a divorced woman was seen as a failure not only as a wife, but as a human being. Mother's worth as a person was dependent on her ability to be a good wife—good, meaning compliant.

Despite Daddy's mistakes, I still adored him and sometimes just wanted him all to myself. After all, he was my first love, like a god on earth. I had absolute bliss when I got special time with him. But that didn't happen often enough, and maybe I needed a little more attention and affection than the rest of my siblings. Between Daddy's multiple offspring and his substantial business dealings, there simply wasn't enough special time to go around.

My unmet craving for affection made me come to a scary realization: even though Mother was a good wife and nurturer, Daddy strayed anyway. If he could do that to her, there was little hope I'd be able to find, satisfy, and keep a man who would love only me.

Stubbornly, I pushed that pessimistic notion deep into my mind and focused on an antithetical idea. I made myself believe that there was a man … somewhere … who would love and cherish only me. It was just a matter of finding him.

Chapter 2

*S*ome people think that the devil arrives in a fiery cloud, accompanied by the putrid smell of brimstone. However, I learned that he often comes as a seductive serpent, adept at shedding whatever skin he is wearing and growing an entirely different one to match the desires of his prey. I found this out in the summer of 1977, when I was eleven years old.

I was working with my sister behind the counter of one of Daddy's several pharmacies. An imposing man entered and cockily strode toward me with his colleagues trailing behind him. That twenty-one-year-old man had a soaring height and was very well built. I was so bashful and intimidated by his stature that I avoided looking at him directly. However, when I did manage to cast my eyes toward his, I was thrown off balance by his piercing stare.

Then, the man began firing a blitzkrieg of questions at me about medicine. Not waiting for me to answer, he audaciously helped himself to the medicine box and perused its stock like I wasn't even there. Out of the corner of my eye, I looked at my uncle, who was also working at the pharmacy. I knew if I let the stranger continue rummaging through the medicine, I'd be in trouble.

I was shy but managed to muster up some courage. I said, "You aren't allowed to open the box. Either buy the medicine or give it back."

Surprised at my attempt at boldness, the man narrowed his eyes as he offered me a fabricated grin, adjusting his approach.

His body language morphed as he went from being pompous to charming. This deviltry was difficult for an unsuspecting person—such as I was—to understand. He said pleasantly, "She has grown up."

The man spoke as if he had knowledge of me while one of his companions nodded in agreement. The man boldly took out a piece of paper and wrote his name and address on it. He forced it into my hand, and I put it in my pocket without even thinking. I didn't want any adult seeing me take that paper; adults had the cultural right to rebuke me and report my misdeed back to my parents. Also, I was intimidated by the man who'd just given the paper to me. I had no idea how he'd react if I rejected his advances on the spot.

Later, I found a private nook so that I could read the paper. I must admit I had been thinking about the mystery man throughout the day, and my interest was piqued. I took a quick peek to make sure no one was around and unfolded the paper. The man's name was Walter, and the letters EFO were written after it. I had no idea what that meant. So, in the most nonchalant way, I decided to ask a coworker; the last thing I wanted was to arouse her suspicion. She said that it was a military officer training school in another region.

Oh well, I thought. I didn't need to bother myself because I probably would never see Walter again; he was so very far away.

My uneventful life went on. Summer freedom faded away and school resumed. Around this time, I started reading Harlequin Romance novels and joined other teen girls in a book club. The books' plotlines were basically the same. They featured a heroine who fell in love with a man she hated, but somehow, they'd end up living happily ever after. The stories resonated with me because that was what I craved so much: the incorruptible love and attention of a man.

Also, around this time, I saw my sister getting a large amount of attention from pen pals she met through a magazine called *Kouakou*. This made me jealous. And since we were only one year apart, it brought out my competitive side.

One day, it just so happened that I was cleaning out my closet and found that little piece of paper Walter had given me. That was it! Walter could be my pen pal. Even though I was much too young to have a Harlequin Romance hero, I could still have an innocent friendship with Walter. The bonuses would be the extra attention I was missing and, unlike my sister's pals, the fact that Walter was a grown man; she couldn't stop that.

The letter I wrote Walter was short. I reintroduced myself and focused on why he decided to go to military school. I asked one of my sisters how to mail the letter, and off it went. About a month later, Daddy called from downstairs, "Celine, you have mail!"

With an excited gasp, I ran downstairs to retrieve my letter, practically sliding across the marble floor. My pride rose with every slippery step I took, so glad that I had finally one-upped my sister. Daddy was busy looking through his own mail as he handed me mine. I looked at the envelope; there was no return address. Daddy must've assumed it was a regular pen pal letter from an adolescent.

But I knew Walter didn't disclose that the letter came from a military base on account of the army's dishonorable reputation. In most central African countries, soldiers are considered to be the equivalent of criminals. Their temperaments are violent and miserable, and they are also known to be rapists and drug pushers. They are considered a rogue class, and no sane parent wants their children to join them, let alone enter into a romantic relationship with one of them.

Nevertheless, my enthusiasm brimmed as I ran back to my room. I didn't even savor the moment. I ripped the letter open like it was a longed-for Christmas gift. To my surprise, unlike the one I sent Walter, the letter was quite long. But instead of a friendly pen pal letter like the ones my sister got, this letter started off with amorous words like "Cherie" and "Honey." Smirking, I looked at the photo he'd sent with it. Walter was so ugly that he was ten steps past homely.

I quickly took out a pen and a piece of paper and responded. I wrote that I didn't appreciate him calling me romantic nicknames and how his picture would've caused me problems if Daddy had decided to inspect the letter before giving it to me. Moreover, I changed my mind and no longer wanted anything to do with a lowlife military man.

Instead of leaving me be, Walter wrote back apologizing and explaining his reasons for joining the army. He said he would be returning to my town in the summer. But the creepy part of the letter said that he had been praying about me and knew I was his wife.

To an eleven-year-old girl, those kinds of words coming from a grown man were disgusting. I was in no way mature enough to deal with Walter's adult advances, but because of my age and culture, I felt it was only respectful to write him back. I did so a couple of times. After I got Walter's intense responses, I stopped.

For the rest of the year, I watched with envy as my sister continued to receive her pen pal letters. It was hard on my ego, but I was consoled by the one thing that gave me enjoyment: my collection of Harlequin Romance novels. Even though I didn't have a steady pen pal, at least I could lose myself in an imaginary hero who would give me the validation and attention I needed.

ime passed. I was thirteen, and once again working at Daddy's pharmacy, which was within walking distance from our house. Since I had proven that I could responsibly go back and forth between the pharmacy and home, Daddy also allowed me to walk around the town. I relished the freedom.

One particular evening, I was walking with my aunt, my mother's sister. She was fifteen years older than me but considered cool; I could talk to her about anything. As we meandered, I just so happened to notice a handsome man in a military uniform standing next to another gentleman. The handsome man kept looking at me, and I admit that he had caught my eye, too.

"Look at that good-looking man over there," I whispered with jitters in my stomach. As my aunt and I continued toward the handsome man, I thought it was too bad Walter didn't look like him.

The men started to follow us after we passed. I looked over my shoulder, and the handsome man was eyeballing me so hard that I could feel the weight of his stare. The jitters disappeared and were replaced by lead because now I felt vulnerable and exposed. I wanted to get away from him as quickly as I could and subtly motioned for my aunt to walk faster. But it seemed like we were walking in slow motion.

Scared, I kept looking back; however, I couldn't help but think how attractive the handsome stranger was. He looked like he belonged on the cover of a Harlequin Romance novel.

His midnight-colored skin covered a majestic body, the perfect hanger for his crisp uniform. His face was chiseled and alluring.

"Celine?" the man blurted out. "Are you Celine or Celine's sister?"

The man's question didn't surprise me. My sister and I were close in age and highly resembled each other.

"I'm Celine. Who are you?" I asked timidly.

"I thought you'd remember my name. It's Walter," he said with absolute charisma.

The shock left me dumbfounded for a moment. Was this the same ugly guy in the picture? As soon as my mind came back, I walked away as fast as I could with my aunt in tow. I didn't know what else to do. When we gained enough distance to be totally out of Walter's sight, I told her how happy I was to see him again. I had no worries over telling her because I knew she would keep the secret.

As soon as I got home, I frantically searched for Walter's photograph. I found it and remembered how I had shown it to my sisters and cousins. We all laughed because he was looking hideous. Little did I know that the photograph was the image of Walter's true character, not the window-dressed man I saw in uniform that day.

Unable to see the future, I believed Walter's phantasmal projection of a knight in shining armor, and I wanted to see him again. But I had not stopped long enough to talk to him. He didn't even have my address. How could my hero possibly find me again? I sadly accepted that I had let the opportunity pass.

But fate had other plans. About a week later, I had the rare opportunity to stand outside the family compound by myself. Against the backdrop of the horizon, a figure was coming toward me with purpose; it was Walter. My feet shuffled as I tried to decide between welcoming Walter and going back inside; in no way did I want my parents to see me with him when they returned. However, curiosity decided for me and firmly planted me in place.

Walter reached me and was no respecter of personal space, standing mere inches away. He emanated peculiar energy that frightened yet tantalized me. However, I didn't move. Instead, I craned my neck to look up at him and asked, "How did you know where I lived?"

"I asked around. I passed your house many times hoping I would see you. I guess today is *your* lucky day," Walter said with a cocky grin.

"My parents will be home at any moment. I can't talk to you," I said on the lookout for my folks.

"I have a sister who lives nearby. We could meet at her house and have a nice talk."

My intuition was screaming at me to run away. However, I agreed and we set up a time to meet. But how was I going to get out of the house? I hated to lie, but Walter's handsomeness overcame my reservations. I decided that I would leave the house under the pretense of studying with a girlfriend, Helen.

Because my parents liked Helen, it was easy to deceive them. They allowed me to have a little more freedom for the sake of my education. I swore Helen to secrecy, and my clandestine meetings with Walter began.

The provocative dew of first love left me inebriated, and I made sure to lap up every drop. I eagerly looked forward to the heady rush of adrenaline that occurred every time I sneaked away from home. Every moment Walter and I were together, the world seemed to be enveloped in a dreamy haze where illusion was a reality. The newness of Walter's kisses and touches were the most amazing sensations I'd ever experienced. In addition, since I had just entered my teens, the surge of hormones exacerbated my reactions.

The more time I spent with Walter, the more I believed he was my Harlequin Romance lover. He wanted to know everything about me and was so attentive to my needs.

In conjunction with his ability to sway my emotions and libido, he used marriage as a lure to pull me deeper into an abyss.

Walter eventually wanted more frequent get-togethers, which forced me to lie to my parents more. I felt wrenching guilt. But I was so much in love, it didn't matter. However, even though I was totally in love, sometimes Walter did make me feel uneasy, especially when he made suggestions about my clothing choices. He would give me other small criticisms in the form of helpful hints. He also started to monitor my activities when we weren't together. He constantly wanted to know where I was and who I was with.

I balked occasionally but usually acquiesced to make him happy, and I was more than glad to do it. When it came to Walter, my situational awareness was nonexistent. Because of that, Walter shrewdly knew how much overt control to display during the early stages of our relationship. He was aware that if there was too much, I'd cut ties. But the day did come when he was very comfortable and didn't mind exposing his fangs.

On that particular day, for some unknown reason, Walter was vexed. It was like there was a hurricane gusting behind his eyes. He menacingly hovered over me and proclaimed, "If you ever leave me, I *will* kill you. I promise."

Though most girls would've cringed at Walter's announcement, it made me swoon. I was aroused by his fervency. I took his possessiveness and dangerous words as proof of his love.

My mind flickered briefly to thoughts about my parents. Daddy never made a "promise" to Mother the way Walter had just done to me. Maybe that passion … that heat … was missing from my parents' relationship. Maybe the threat of death is what it took to have that special love—the kind of love someone would kill for.

I fell into Walter's arms, elated. I hungrily clutched him with total devotion as I tried to meld my body with his. I finally had the extraordinary and exclusive love that I longed for. From then on, not only my body, but my heart and soul were pledged to him.

Chapter 4

I continued to secretly see Walter. Though the process was gradual, he came to see me as property; but, I was the property that didn't belong to him. As long as I was a teenager living in Daddy's house as his daughter, Daddy owned me.

This thought was intolerable to Walter, who sought total control. He pushed me to reveal our relationship to Daddy, but I absolutely refused to. There was no way I was going to confess my misdeeds to my beloved Daddy.

However, Walter was an adept military strategist and combated my resistance like he would in any war. He decided to invade by deploying a sneak attack on Daddy. He went to Daddy's office and exposed our relationship.

Initially, Daddy thought Walter was one of my sister's pen pals but was shocked and dismayed when he understood Walter was talking about me. Though Walter tried to make our relationship sound innocent, his words still were like napalm, and Daddy's heart took the spray.

Daddy was no fool and knew what was really going on. He couldn't believe that not only had I betrayed his trust, but I did it with a military deviant ... me, his beloved *mundele net a rater*.

Walter, on the other hand, was satisfied because his will would be served no matter how the situation panned out. He had successfully driven an emotional wedge between Daddy and me. If Daddy forbade me to see Walter, Walter knew I would do whatever it took to continue our sordid affair. If Daddy conceded, Walter essentially was procuring property—me.

Meanwhile, I was informed of Walter's action. I knew I was in trouble and tried to pray myself into invisibility. I paced the floor as I waited for Daddy to come home, knowing that I would see a side of him I'd never seen before … one filled with wrath against me.

Soon enough, I heard Daddy's car door slam. My breathing quickened at the sound of the front door creaking open. Sweat broke out of my pores as Daddy's footsteps got closer to my bedroom. Moments later, I could see Daddy's shadow at the bottom of the closed door. He just stood there for a while, hesitating. I wished he would've just gotten my annihilation over with.

I watched Daddy come in. But instead of seeing the rage on his face, I saw sorrow. I was prepared for anger but not sorrow. Sorrow was worse.

"Your friend visited me today," Daddy said calmly. "He said that he's your pen pal. Is that true?"

I nodded as I hid my eyes. I could tell that Daddy knew Walter was more than a pen pal. With shame, I lied and said, "Yes."

Daddy drew in a breath and sat on my bed next to me. I knew he hoped that I would've given him a different answer. He said, "I'm disappointed in you. But I know if you went through all the trouble to see this man, there is nothing I can do to keep you from him."

Tears welled up in my eyes, and not because I got caught. It was because of what I had done to Daddy. I wanted so badly to go back in time, before I met Walter, to prevent the pain Daddy was going through.

Daddy was deep in thought for a few moments and then said, "Let's go for a ride. I want to show you something."

As Daddy headed to the car, I realized our relationship was permanently changed. We were now two different people to each other. I was the betrayer, and he was the betrayed. But maybe, for a change, he finally felt the way Mother did.

Daddy took me to an outdoor market. It was a sad place populated by poor women selling wares, produce, and meat just to get a few measly francs. Despite the utter poverty and dead-end atmosphere, the women still somehow managed to give off a glow. This glow came from a faith that things could get better, and for some of them, that pitiful market was actually better than where they'd come from.

I couldn't stop squirming in my seat. I wasn't used to being around poor people, and the thick tension between Daddy and me made things even worse. I wanted to go home and separate myself from the market and Daddy as soon as possible.

As we continued on, Daddy pointed out a young woman. She had a delightful face and a lithe body. The way she moved hinted at some sophistication. Physically, she had enough appeal to be the trophy wife of a prominent man. But she was stuck in the grimy market instead.

"See that girl," Daddy said. "She's very pretty. Today she seems radiant like she has sunlight beaming from her soul. However, she is here in this market like all the rest of these women. What put her in this place? Choices. We don't know what choices she made that caused her to be in that stand. The same goes for you. All the choices you make will affect your life. Is Walter … *your pen pal* … what you still choose?"

I finally told the truth. "Yes, Daddy."

"It looks like you've made your choice. I have lived my life, and you'll have to live yours. But you know you'll have to accept everything that comes with being with that man."

Daddy drove us back home. On the way, Daddy told me that he was still my father and would lay down some ground rules. If I wanted to see Walter, he would have to come over to the compound for proper dates. This was not an offer of generosity. It was really a way for Daddy to monitor Walter and me. In-house visits would let Daddy see whether Walter displayed any "militaristic" tendencies and reduce the possibility of Walter violating me. Unfortunately, regarding the latter, it was too late.

I hated it when Walter came to our house to visit. His presence being there was proof of my chicanery, and his arrival always aroused my guilt. Moreover, Walter was out of place. It was like mixing oil and water when it came to Walter and my siblings and our same-aged friends. They were high school kids and Walter was a soldier in his mid-twenties; they had absolutely nothing in common. Daddy was also lurking about the house, making sure nothing salacious was going on. But I dealt with it because I was so in love with Walter … my hero.

Time slowly passed, and my high school graduation was approaching. I was engrossed in studying for my finals and contemplating the life after high school. Walter was already making plans for me, though.

"I'm going to ask your father to let my parents come over to your house," Walter informed me.

I swallowed hard. That was a sure sign of a marriage proposal. Happiness rose in my belly, and the largest smile I ever had stretched across my face. I could see a perfect life laid out before me. I'd graduate from high school, go to college, and be married to the most committed man on earth. All that was missing was a horse for the two of us to ride off into the sunset.

As expected, my parents were reluctant to extend an invitation to Walter's father and step-mother, but they did so anyway. The night the two sets of parents met, they kept a chasm between them as they sat across from each other in our living room. They listened to Walter's proposal, and no one was pleased.

Walter's step-mother was particularly prickly. She had replaced Walter's biological mother after his parents' divorce and physically abused him when he was very young. Consequently, Walter blamed his real mother for letting the abuse happen and abandoning him.

What young Walter did not know was that his real mother tried everything she could to keep him in her life. However, based on folkways, she was not only banned from seeing him, but also had a curse put on her. The curse would bring harm to Walter if she ever tried to contact or help him in any way.

But on the night of my engagement, I couldn't see the negative impact that Walter's two mothers had on him and how it was going to affect me later on. In my mind, that night was strictly about my engagement and parental disapproval, and the long-dead history didn't matter a bit to me. Nothing and no one would stop me from being Walter's wife.

Chapter 5

*I*f I hadn't been so in love and immature, I would've seen the omens leading up to my wedding day in 1985.

During the engagement, everyone around me was a human crystal ball. No one expressed any joy or congratulatory sentiments. In fact, most people were aghast upon hearing the news about the upcoming nuptials.

Peter, our family friend, winced whenever the much-dreaded wedding was mentioned. He had watched me change over the years due to my involvement with Walter. To Peter, the sweet and confident girl he knew while growing up was now an elusive memory. I had morphed into a deluded woman driven by a tempestuous love. Peter never talked to me about it, but he discussed it with other concerned Sunday school pals.

My parents were simply depressed about the engagement. During the wedding planning, my parents questioned me about my intentions and told me that it was not too late to back out. Neighbors added to their distress by constantly asking them why they were letting me marry Walter. Mother's sisters believed Walter somehow wrapped me up spiritually and had me hypnotized. It was almost as if God was sending people to my parents to block the marriage.

But I was hell-bent on becoming a Mrs., and there was nothing my parents could do about it. I had graduated from high school and was supposedly old enough to make my own decisions. Thus, it was clear to me that everyone else was delusional. They had to be if they couldn't see the profound love that Walter and I shared. They were just jaded naysayers who lacked happiness in their own love lives and couldn't see the beauty in mine. Obviously, they were jealous or just wanted to keep me down.

They had no idea how determined I was to be Walter's wife. I was also determined to avoid a destiny like Mother's. Unlike her, I would not only be strong and independent, but I would also have a faithful husband. I had no limitations with Walter by my side.

Indeed, Walter had his ways. I reasoned, however, that his possessiveness and critical attitude were only signs that he loved me and wanted me to be the best I could be. I thought with Walter's love and careful guidance, I could only expand.

The wedding drew closer. Walter and I were subjected to advice given by not only my parents, but also the elders, and the women in particular. In reality, these words of wisdom were more for me than him. The recurring sentiments were that there was to be no dissolution of the marriage regardless of what Walter did, and I was always expected to submit. I listened but didn't feel that the advice pertained to me. I respectfully informed the elder women that Walter was going to be a good husband, and I wouldn't have a reason to basically endure the marriage. They looked at each other knowingly and told me that I'd see.

My parents carried on with tradition and showed me my bedroom. Daddy said, "Celine, once you are Walter's wife, this room is no longer available to you. You'll be his wife, and his home is where you'll stay."

Fear caused me to shudder like it was a frigid breeze on my skin. I was not privy to all the rites of passage that adults were aware of, so I took Daddy's symbolic words literally. I believed I was permanently ousted as a resident of my childhood home. Did this same scenario happen to Mother? Still not understanding Mother's true motivation, I wondered if this was why she stayed married.

I couldn't help but feel like my safety net was gone—that my parents were abandoning me. My misguided logic told me that I had to make sure my marriage worked, not only out of love, but of necessity because I had nowhere else to go. Marrying Walter meant giving up so much, but he was worth it.

The cynics didn't win, and I finally recited marriage vows to Walter. My parents sat in the front row weeping and praying because of the disaster they witnessed. Walter victoriously eyeballed me, the spoils of war he took from Daddy.

When we were pronounced man and wife, I was blissfully connected to the man of my dreams. I looked at the witnesses who were clapping only out of politeness. Next, I turned toward my parents for validation. Daddy couldn't even manage a somber smile. Mother just shook her head with disappointment.

Later, Daddy approached Walter. Daddy said, "I know it can be a struggle for a young couple starting out. I'd like to offer you and Celine some money and furniture."

Walter was very much a tribal man and had no use for the Christian and family values Daddy upheld. Walter relied on paternalistic and misogynistic standards when it came to marital relations. He knew that if he took the money, he would be beholden to Daddy. He was too proud to be under another man.

Daddy's gifts also would have meant that I was still under his rule. Walter needed to sever as many of my ties to Daddy as he could and be my sole owner. Separating me from my family and isolating me were the first steps in a systematic process to make me totally dependent on Walter, not only financially, but emotionally as well.

Walter stood straighter to add the illusion of more height to his already tall frame. He looked down his nose at Daddy and said, "No. Celine and I can survive on our own. Whatever money I make will suffice."

Daddy looked at me. "Celine, what do you say?" Daddy asked. His eyes were begging me to take him up on his offer.

I looked at Walter and then Daddy. "Daddy, we don't need it. We'll be fine," I said.

"Have it your way," Daddy said as he walked away. He maintained his dignity, but his heavy shoulders exposed the grief and fear he felt in giving me over to Walter.

As I was leaving with my husband, Mother and my aunts sang a woeful song. The lyrics spoke of going through your life and seeing it as a journey brought to you by God and that there would be trials but remember to pray earnestly.

I didn't pay much attention to their singing at the time; I was too enraptured by Walter. However, the song turned out to be a warning. God was preparing me by giving me something to keep in my mind—though in its recesses—for my journey ahead.

Chapter 6

$\mathscr{I}$t was not long after the wedding that signs of trouble appeared. African families expect brides to become pregnant immediately after their weddings. However, I still had not conceived several months after mine.

Walter was convinced my eighteen-year-old womb was the problem and blamed me entirely. He tried to steer me toward visiting a backcountry witch doctor for some aphrodisiacal herbs and a magical fertility ritual for good measure.

I still had my pride at that point and staunchly refused his ridiculous suggestion. My rebelliousness toward Walter's dark-sided superstition put him on notice. He foresaw that he'd have to exert more control in the future if he wanted to maintain his position as the head of our union.

Thank goodness Walter's strife with the army diverted some of his attention away from me. He was suspected of being a member of the Tshisekedi Movement, a group opposed to the Joseph Mobutu regime, the dictatorial government at the time. They thought he could've been a spy and traitor, like some sort of sleeper. Even though he served eleven years, he was never promoted above the rank of lieutenant, because of this suspicion. In fact, it was a common occurrence for army members from the same region as Etienne Tshisekedi, like Walter, to be denied any promotion in rank. Walter even tried to attend college, but the army wouldn't release him and forced him to continue to serve as some sort of punishment.

Eventually, Walter was stationed in the remote frontier at the border of Zaire and Angola. This was the front line of an ongoing conflict, and we both believed Walter was sent there in retaliation for his possible connection to the Tshise-kedi Movement.

I accompanied Walter to his various mission posts. Our movement was constant, and we had to get to Walter's posts the best way we could. We'd usually travel at night by hopping on some rickety bus filled beyond capacity with tired, sweaty riders. The concentrated smell of human stench was unbearable.

Whatever bus we were on would continue for some miles until the pavement stopped, and then we had to walk the rest of the way. We traversed thick jungle areas where women were actually forbidden to go by army decree. We often found ourselves crossing over some sort of danger-ous makeshift bridge or navigating a rushing waterway that was waiting to swallow us up. We learned to trek barely vis-ible dirt paths hidden by prickly bushes. If there was no path, guides cleared thorny shrubs that harbored poisonous snakes and other dangerous critters. When we did manage to find a hint of civilization, it was usually a primitive village or haunting cemetery with macabre stick-crosses marking the deceased.

There was never a time I wasn't afraid while traveling. I wished I was back at my parents' home and living the life of luxury I was accustomed to. But I was told I could never go back and had to take everything that my marriage to Walter brought me. So far, my romantic marriage had bestowed swollen feet covered with pus-filled blisters from all the hik-ing, and they had to heal on their own because there was no medication to be found.

One of my military homes was a mud hut. I had to light it up with a kerosene lantern. However, sometimes Walter would take the lantern when he left for his graveyard shift.

That's when I was left alone in the dark. The only thing I could do was try to get some rest on my handcrafted cot made of palm leaves. However, I couldn't sleep because of the filthy pigs scratching their backs on the outside of the hut, causing clay particles to fall all over me.

I spent most nights praying and crying. In an attempt not to go crazy, I tried to look at the ordeals as adventures. When that didn't work, I tried to convince myself that I was satisfied because at least I had Walter.

During one of those adventures, Walter and I arrived at a remote military camp where I was the only woman. I felt like a lamb surrounded by a pack of wicked, hungry wolves. The soldiers were unpredictable, and I had no idea what they'd do to me when Walter wasn't around. I wasn't the only one disturbed by their presence. The citizens of the surrounding villages also saw them as threats. However, the villages had to tolerate the soldiers because they needed military protection from rebels from neighboring countries.

I was lucky that the soldiers left me alone, but others weren't so fortunate. The soldiers had absolutely no sexual restraint. Because they couldn't bring their women as Walter did, their lusts sent them to the villages, where they would rape girls.

The rapes became so frequent and violent that the village chiefs asked the shamans to decree curses on any soldiers caught in such heinous acts. The hexes supposedly would make the rapists' penises shrivel and fall off.

But the soldiers found a loophole; they pretended to marry the girls. That way, the men could subjugate the girls to whatever sexual aberrances they wanted to. However, they promptly abandoned the girls when their military stints were over. The girls were left used up, diseased, and pregnant. They were shunned by others in the villages and became outcasts.

Being a commander's wife, the rapes weren't part of my everyday experience, and I could easily distance myself from them. I had no understanding of the pain and trauma that was inflicted on those young women. I figured as long as the soldiers weren't bothering me, all was well. Besides, Walter never rebuked his soldiers. I started thinking, *How bad could they be?*

I had no idea that Walter was also abusing those girls. It never clicked until I was on the receiving end—when he started abusing me.

Chapter 7

I could see dissatisfaction rising up in Walter. Something was eating him up inside. Of course, I thought that Walter's unhappiness fell on me because I was the wife. I brooded over what I may have done or was not doing that could've been contributing to his funk.

Adding to Walter's despondency was the fact that he wasn't being promoted. I knew he'd seen the nice homes and cars that soldiers of higher ranks were getting. It was a slam to his pride to come home to our mediocre abode, and his resentfulness made him curse it.

It was on me to relieve the burden that having a wife had put on Walter. I enrolled in Mbanza-Ngungu Teacher Training College. This decision was not based only on my desire to help Walter. It was also because I came from an educated and achievement-oriented family. I wanted to carry out my familial custom and, if God saw fit, also be a role model for my future children by showing them the benefits of knowledge and effort. I majored in English, as that was all that was available at the time.

My enrollment in the university stoked Walter's inner conflicts and left him double-minded. He knew I'd outpace him, therefore highlighting his failures and inadequacies. But he couldn't deny the material benefits my degree would bring, so his covetousness of other soldiers' wealth compelled him to tolerate my studies.

However, it would be years before I would receive my degree. Walter's green-eyed monster couldn't wait that long to be fed; so, one day, Walter brought home a big sack.

"We're about to be rich," Walter said.

Walter threw the sack on the table and opened it like Santa's bag. As I made my way to the sack, I felt evil seeping from it. Carefully, I peeked inside and saw bricks of marijuana. I looked back with disbelief at Walter standing there like he had actually done something worthwhile. I swept the sack filled with sin away from me.

"You have to get that out of here. We don't need money that bad," I said as I wiped the sack's taint off my hands.

Walter walked over to me and pointed his finger directly at my face. "It's just like you to think so small. I'm the man, and I say, it stays here. And, don't you even think about touching it."

I remembered what the elders said about marriage: that I was to submit to Walter. Since Walter would not listen to me, all I could do was pray that sack away. Shortly after that, Walter gave the sack to a cousin, who lived in the area, to sell the drugs for him. That didn't happen because the cousin disappeared with the loot. I had prayed those drugs away.

Walter's and my relationship started to show more signs of strain. Walter's criticisms of me turned into all-out disapproval. We bickered more, but somehow, I knew how far I should let my anger rise.

I found solace at school. In one of my classes, the professor taught us the song "We Shall Overcome." The melody and message resonated with me and seemed like something nice to sing to my children one day. But just like the song Mother and my aunts sang to me, it foretold that more troubles headed my way.

But the troubles would have to wait. Blessedly, God heard more of my prayers and brought some much-needed happiness into my life.

I had been suffering from what I thought was a stomach bug. Since the water at the military base was not the best, I attributed it to a simple bacterial infection. I decided to go to the doctor for tests. However, those blood tests came back negative. Then as a precautionary measure, a urine test was done.

The doctor came in with the results. "Celine, I have something to report," said the doctor, smiling. "You're pregnant."

Pregnant, really? I thought, my eyes twinkling with awe. My maternal instinct kicked in, and my hand naturally caressed my belly that was filled with an unseen miracle.

The months that followed seemed like an eternity, and I finally delivered the baby. The nurse handed the tiny stranger to me. The baby and I introduced ourselves to each other with mutual glances. I took note of his details, like how his face was all squished up. His pinkish skin was covered with downy hair and wrinkled like the folds in a bedsheet. The baby looked more like an alien than a human. He was absolutely gorgeous!

As I marveled at the wonder nestled in my arms, I pondered how a newborn could possess so much calmness. How could something so tranquil ... so perfect ... come from me? He was peace incarnate. I swear, even though I had love for Walter, my love for my son eclipsed it by a thousand times.

The newborn baby, Solomon, was now the love of my life.

Chapter 8

The Mobutu regime enjoyed friendly relationships with several American Republican presidents. Through these diplomatic connections, Zaire received tremendous financial support and aid from the United States. The United States, in turn, had an ally against communism and was eager to train Congolese soldiers toward that end.

In 1990, Walter was sent to the United States—Georgia, specifically—for specialized military training. I was proud of his achievement, and my ego was stroked by being his wife. Though we were having personal problems, I could brush them aside because Walter was acting out the part of my romantic hero.

Before Walter left for the States, I found out I was pregnant with our second child. During Walter's absence, I sometimes felt lonely and cheated out of having my husband's support during my pregnancy. But I at least had Solomon and thoughts of the new baby to buoy my spirit.

I didn't think it would be possible to love another child as much as I loved Solomon … until Hannah was born. Hannah was long and big, taking after her father. Her Kewpie doll face acted like a magnet making her utterly irresistible.

Immediately after Hannah's birth, I called Walter. Cradling the baby in my arms, I softly said, "Walter, we have a daughter."

I paused, waiting for him to ask about our well-being. When I didn't hear anything, with curtness I said, "We are fine."

Matter-of-factly, Walter asked, "Is she beautiful?"

I found that to be an odd question, the coldness of it. Totally bewildered, I responded, "Yes, gorgeous."

Walter's sigh of relief rattled me. I hung up with him as soon as I could and focused on my daughter. I immediately noticed how Hannah was similar to Solomon as far as a peaceful temperament was concerned, but I sensed something else about her—delicate sweetness.

In my arms was a child destined to spend her childhood being a mother figure to those she cared for; in fact, we ended up nicknaming her Big Momma.

After the birth, life went on. I felt like a struggling, single mother due to Walter's absence. I was so relieved when my folks allowed me and the children to temporarily live with them. As soon as the invitation was extended, my bags were practically packed. A sumptuous environment, delicious food, and my parents' doting attention were all waiting for me. Finally, I would be taken care of instead of having to take care of someone for a change. Those few months at home ended up being some of the lightest and freest I've had in my entire life.

Daddy offered me the opportunity to work at his pharmaceutical factory, and I jumped right on it. I had been itching for a chance to become a professional woman, someone of importance. Since nepotism was not something Daddy was interested in, he let me know that I'd to work from the bottom to the top. I wouldn't be his daughter in the workplace and would have to prove I was worthy of working there like everyone else. I didn't mind, though. I was eager to test myself, to see what I could achieve by using my intellect and talents.

While working at the factory, I realized how much of myself I'd lost in the short time I had been married to Walter. Working helped me to remember that I was a sophisticated, brilliant, and witty woman who had so much to contribute to the world. Also, as my inner self grew more robust, it was reflected in my clothing choices. No longer was I restricted to wearing plain clothes that I had to settle for due to budgetary restrictions. I was now a working woman who slipped into finely tailored garments that were more natural to me.

I had earned my way to a managerial position when a letter arrived from Walter in 1991. It said that he was planning to desert the military and remain in the United States. His reason was that he feared further persecution due to his supposed connection to the Tshisekedi Movement. He urged me to leave and join him before he was due to come back home.

My family and I were already familiar with government intrusion. Because of our tribe and the region of our births, we always had some kind of monitoring. I remember when we tried to go on vacation out of the country. To do that, as residents of Zaire, we needed special permission to leave. When Daddy applied for us, he was denied. Immediately after the denial, Mobutu sent armed soldiers to stand guard outside our family compound for over a month and seized radio equipment that they thought Daddy might've been using for the opposition movement.

That experience let me know that the government kept a list of people who were not allowed to leave the country. As the wife of a suspected Tshisekedi supporter, my black-list status doubled, and I definitely would not be allowed to leave, even though the government had yet to find out about Walter's plan to flee the army.

I looked down at Solomon playing on the floor and Hannah sleeping in her bassinet. Not only was Walter putting my life in danger, but our babies' lives as well. If I stayed in Zaire, the moment the government found out that Walter had abandoned the army, they would first take my children and then hold me hostage. Then, if Walter didn't return to

Africa out of fear for his personal safety, I may have been killed. So, it was not a matter of wanting to go to the States, but a life-saving necessity.

Still, I kept rereading Walter's letter, hoping that I read it wrong. But the words never changed. As I thought about Walter's decision, anger toward him supplanted my fear. Once again because of Walter, I would have to say goodbye to the happiness and safety of home. So far, none of Walter's decisions had brought me any real benefit, and now his actions threatened to destroy whatever little good we had.

But I could hear the voices of the elders. I tried to shut them out, but they were like incessant ringing in the ears. They offered me no alternatives and only reminded me that this is what I chose. The voices said, "You were cautioned. You were warned. These are the consequences of your desire for that man. Deal with it."

Chapter 9

*W*hen I was a teen, my parents offered to send me to an exclusive school in Belgium. Most young women would've jumped at the chance to be away from parental supervision in an exotic land. Not me.

I never had wanderlust. Why would I? Everything that I needed and that made me happy was in Zaire. My parents, siblings, and culture were more than sources of delight; they were the three pillars of my support system. I staunchly refused my parents' offer in order to remain in the loving environment that had nurtured me. I just knew that I'd stay in Zaire for the rest of my life, even if Mobutu was in charge.

But Walter's decision to desert the army changed all of that permanently. I had to flee Zaire because I was about to be a fugitive—an official enemy of the state with my fellow countrymen coming for me at any time. But first, I needed to get a passport.

To obtain a passport, I had to use my wits along with any connections I had. I only had one option, a friend who worked for the Ministry of Foreign Affairs in Lubumbashi. I hesitantly contacted him. I knew the seriousness of what I was asking for, but he courageously agreed to help me.

My friend and I didn't have a network we could rely on; we were just two people secretly bucking the government. We were putting both our lives in jeopardy and were terrified. But there was nothing else that could be done.

At work, my friend kept up a front, always pretending like he was performing ordinary office tasks. But he was really searching endless files for a name, and one day, he found one. It allowed us to forge the documents so I could obtain an alias, a passport, and a visitor's visa from the United States consulate in Lubumbashi. When I went to pick up the documents, I tracked every corner of the building, fully expecting the authorities to descend upon me.

Arrangements for my trip to the United States were made, and the journey was awful. I was nervous, spooked. It seemed as though all eyes were on me. At every stop, I looked over my shoulder, anticipating that law enforcement would give chase and take me in. Anytime someone suddenly appeared next to me, I jumped three feet off the ground.

I also thought about Walter as I sat at various international airports. I resented him for being safe in the United States and not having to make any sort of familial sacrifice. Since he was not as loyal to his family as I was to mine, it was easier for him to make the choice to stay in the United States, regardless of the situation. When it came to the extended family, he really wasn't losing anything.

Moreover, even though Walter was in training and couldn't leave his post, it frustrated me that all he had to do was wait for me and the children to arrive. I, on the other hand, had to go through the ordeal of escaping Zaire with two little ones in tow.

Walter loved me ... I assumed. Nevertheless, I condemned him silently. As I flew over the Atlantic Ocean, I wondered, *Where was my hero? Wasn't Walter supposed to be taking care of me? Why was it on me, the wife, to risk my life to save the family?*

After a long and arduous trip, I arrived at Kennedy Airport on April 7, 1991. Walter was not there to meet me. But to his credit, he didn't officially desert the army while I was still in Africa. He did that for my protection.

I couldn't help but feel so alone and overwhelmed by the radical detour my life had taken, but there was no time to contemplate it. I had to fulfill my duties as a wife and take care of my two babies. I continued on my journey, traveling to Washington, DC, and then to Georgia.

I found that Walter had adjusted to life in the United States quite well. His only qualm was the westernized ways of the women. Their independence and assertiveness were disconcerting to him. However, he was confident that I would never turn into one of those bitter shrews—that I would uphold his tribal beliefs.

One thing that had not happened while Walter was in the States was him becoming a Godly man. When it came to matters of the soul, Walter had his own warped way of thinking, which definitely conflicted with mine. That is what prompted me to join a church as soon as I could. The one I found had a congregation composed of fellow immigrants from Zaire. Because Walter wasn't a believer like me, the church brought a much-needed religious connection to my homeland. I found others like me who offered understanding, comradery, and a sense of belonging that I couldn't have gotten anywhere else in Georgia, or even from Walter.

About a month later, Walter deserted the army. It didn't take long for the government to retaliate. Daddy called to tell me that Zairean troops had been to his home and demanded to know the whereabouts of Walter and me. The troops warned Daddy that when we were found, we would be taken into custody.

Custody meant basic imprisonment at best and torture at worste—unless the government decided to murder you outright. There were stories about men who were taken to underground dungeons where they'd be brutally clobbered with spiked boards. With each excruciating blow, the spikes would penetrate deeply into the flesh, and when the boards were drawn back, bloody pieces of skin and muscle tissue were brought up with them. Also, these poor souls' battered bodies were electrocuted several times a day. The political prisoners' wives weren't spared either. Not only were they in danger of being held hostage and forced to undergo the aforementioned tortures, but also rape—by a single individual or gang—as well.

Walter and I anticipated the soldiers' arrival after my departure and took precautions. We didn't divulge our new address in the United States to anyone in our home country, including our parents. We couldn't risk troops ransacking our families' homes and finding the address randomly written down somewhere. Government loyalists may have been in the United States.

Not only did the Zairean government come after us, but also some of Walter's friends. Several of those friends were killed by Mobutu's forces for suspected involvement in the Tshisekedi Movement just after I left the country. I thought about their mothers and fathers weeping over their graves, lives lost to evil.

I also thought about Daddy and Mother, and this brought me relief. But this was not a comforting relief. It was the woeful realization that one might feel seconds after narrowly avoiding a deadly ten-car pileup on the highway. That feeling arose from knowing just how close Daddy and Mother came to standing over my casket.

Chapter 10

 $\mathcal{W}$ alter and I had a brief honeymoon period after my arrival in the States. I felt safe enough to let my guard down and was enjoying how Walter was acting like a loving husband, though in a way that was consistent with his tribal beliefs. Peace reigned in the home as long as I didn't get unruly in his opinion.

I couldn't see that Walter had a plan for me. His multipoint plan was simple and would be done in progressive steps over a period of years. The first phase—separating me from my family—was already taken care of thanks to the Congolese government. The second phase consisted of Walter giving me false expectations about how our life in America would be. This included making our apartment appear *initially* as a safe haven by juxtaposing it with the danger we escaped from in Africa. He also convinced me that having less in life was somehow a noble way of living—the third phase. The fourth phase was to make me totally dependent on him emotionally and physically. The final phase was total degradation.

Weeks passed. I was adjusting to life in America and found out I was pregnant. Even though Walter's and my situation was not optimal, I was thrilled to know I was carrying another life inside me. But Walter took the news of another baby with a casual air. It was like he was a stud mule who had just done his job.

The longer I was in the States, the more Walter's behavior changed. He had always been a forceful person, but in America, his temperament grew even more aggressive toward me. Fist-sized holes punctured the walls as a result of his ever-increasing tirades. His criticisms about my clothing became hostile demands about what I was going to wear. Malicious insults also spewed from his mouth as he shoved me about.

I tried my best to keep my stress level down for the sake of the baby I was carrying, but Walter made that impossible. That is why I was so glad when Abigail was born, knowing that she wouldn't have to suffer from the strife I was constantly trying to buffer her from. I don't think I would've been able to fight off Walter's onslaughts much longer.

Abigail was a pure expression of love and joy. Her happiness was revealed by a brilliant smile that took over her whole face.

Of course, Walter was proud of his biological achievement. But I felt like he had no right to lay claim to such a blithe creation.

After Abigail's birth, Walter and I had to face yet another hurdle. We had little savings at the time he deserted the army and were under tremendous financial strain. The money ran out, and we couldn't work because of our visitor visas being nonvalid for employment. We decided to enlist the help of US immigration. After we pleaded our case for asylum, the understanding officer gave us work permits that were renewable every year. In the interim, I received WIC so that the children could have proper food to eat. This was a profound blow to Walter's sense of manhood.

I eventually found a job as a housekeeper at a hotel. The housekeeping staff consisted of other immigrants like me and working-class American women. They all had their burdens. Some were struggling with language barriers. Others dealt with lack of opportunity resulting from their limited educations. Despite their challenges, they were a jovial and caring group of women brought together by monetary necessity.

The work was long and tiresome. Vacuuming was the easiest part. The roar of the vacuum was actually quite soothing at times. The next easiest task was making the bed. Every once in a while, I'd find the remnants of lovemaking, but I was going to have to change the sheets anyway. However, the bathroom was the monster. I always sighed as I stepped into bathrooms that had stained, wet towels strewed all over the floor. Sinks were often caked with dried toothpaste and other unrecognizable gunk. But the worst was the toilets. As I scrubbed them down, I had to seriously question some of the guests' home training.

The other maids' and my interactions with guests ran the gamut. Some of the guests had no respect for us. We were invisible to others. Thankfully, there were those who saw us as equals and appreciated our services. Those were the ones who were generous, not only leaving tips but also genuine well-wishes for the future. If I was having a bad day, those well-wishes meant more to me than the tip.

But no matter how we were treated, we all knew that we were integral to the success of the hotel. If the cleanliness was not up to par, nothing else concerning the guests' stays mattered. In that regard, we were more important than the chain's CEO.

By this time, some of my family members had immigrated to the United States. I had kept my job at the hotel a secret from them and my family overseas. However, Daddy had somehow managed to get a passport and came to visit. He happened to catch a glimpse of me in my uniform as I was slipping off to work. Daddy stopped me. He said, "You are working as a housekeeper? What is that about? We have housekeepers; we aren't housekeepers."

I knew Daddy was comparing me to my siblings. They were all upwardly mobile, putting their educations to proper use. They made Daddy proud. Then there was me … the housekeeper. I understood that Daddy couldn't accept his *mundele net a rater* in a position he considered akin to a slave.

It seemed like ever since I got involved with Walter, I had done nothing but let Daddy down.

However, I didn't flinch. I told Daddy that I was willingly working to help Walter, and I was not ashamed of what I had to do. There was no way I was going to let Daddy think that marrying Walter was a mistake. I couldn't let Daddy have the satisfaction of knowing he was right. I was determined to make my marriage a success and also diligently work and live off one paltry paycheck after another.

Then, one day, my supervisor called me in. As I entered her office, I wondered if I had done something wrong and retraced my steps. The supervisor's stoic face gave nothing away. She steepled her fingers and said, "Celine, I want to talk to you about your position here."

Oh no! That sounds like she wants to fire me, I thought. I had to let her know that I wanted my job and started rambling about how much I loved and needed it.

Leaning forward, the supervisor countered, "You don't belong here."

"Do I have a complaint against me? I can't recall having done anything wrong," I said, distressed. I started wiping bursts of sweat off my forehead.

"It's nothing like that. No disrespect to the other housekeepers, but you aren't like them. You speak proper English, more articulately than some Americans. Your application says that you are college educated. Celine, really, this housekeeping job—you're better than this."

I almost didn't hear any of what she said because I was coming down from a near panic attack. "What other jobs are there? I don't know what else to do."

"You can try substitute teaching."

I had no idea what substitute teaching was. The supervisor explained the job and how to get started. I left her office with a seed planted in me that ached to blossom, and I decided to allow that seed to grow into a mighty tree. After all, expansion was one of the reasons I married Walter.

By becoming a substitute teacher, maybe I could prove to my family—especially Daddy—that marrying Walter was a good thing. But how long would I *have* to keep proving that? So far, that was all I was doing because the marriage was proving itself to be the opposite of good.

I didn't want to think about the reality of my marriage anymore. I shut down my logical mind and let my emotional mind take over … like I always did when it came to Walter. I couldn't help it; I loved him, and I thought nothing was going to change that. Once again, I made excuses and convinced myself that we would get stronger and make it through the trials.

Time would change things for the better. It just had to.

Chapter 11

$\mathscr{I}$ started the process to become a substitute teacher. Money was my main motivation, but my desire to impress Daddy was the other. I had to prove to him that Walter and I would make it, that we'd be not only happy but deliriously so.

When I was selected to be an official substitute teacher, I immediately called Daddy to let him know.

"That's good," Daddy said. "You can put your education to proper use."

It was obvious from his tone that he had more respect for teaching than cleaning. However, I still wasn't all that I could be in his opinion. I was groomed to be a professional like my ambitious siblings. Daddy was disappointed that I had fallen short. Even I knew I could've been doing more.

After talking to Daddy, I made a quiet promise to myself that one day I would be an American success story. I had no idea how I would make that happen; I just knew I would. I sensed that my substitute teaching job would somehow play a part in setting up my future. With that in mind, every time I went to work, I thought that I was one day closer to my goal.

But as much as I enjoyed teaching, it couldn't obliterate the overwhelming bills that kept coming in. It wasn't only the low hourly wage that kept our bank account in the negative. I also never knew when I would be called up or how much work I'd be given. Additionally, Walter and I only had one mode of transportation, and he usually had that. Therefore, even getting to work was a hassle.

Having only one car also made it difficult to go to the WIC office. Sometimes, there was no food in the home because I didn't have transportation. Walter, it seemed, was preoccupied with his own agenda and couldn't care less about an empty refrigerator. That would prove to be ironic because an empty refrigerator would be the catalyst for years of brutality.

One day, I opened our beat-up fridge and saw that there was no milk for the children, let alone food. Thankfully, I had an appointment at WIC, so I'd be able to get some much-needed staples. But I didn't have the car. I called a good friend and humbly asked for a ride. Thankfully, she was available and said yes. I was relieved to be getting not only food but also the enjoyable company. Walter had been so gloomy that it started transferring to me.

Walter came home later and saw that there was milk in the refrigerator. He remembered that there had not been any when he left earlier in the day. He knew I had been out and had not asked his permission to go.

The sight of the jug definitely triggered something in Walter. He felt like he lost control over me because I didn't wait on him to be our savior. He was jealous that I had to rely on someone else because he was failing to take care of his family, and whoever took me to the store knew it. Instead of taking responsibility for his lack of care, Walter decided to be devious. He called me into the kitchen.

"Celine, get in the car. We are going to the store to get some food," Walter said.

I looked at Walter standing squarely in front of me. His face was blank, impossible to read. I couldn't figure out why this man, who hadn't given a care about groceries before, was now so interested. My gut told me not to go.

"You know what? I think I'll stay here with the kids. They haven't had their naps yet," I said. I was trying to look as unconcerned as possible; I didn't want to provoke Walter because he was acting so strange.

"No, you're coming with me. I need you to get the food since you are the one on WIC," Walter responded sternly. I knew my place in the marriage and obediently followed Walter's directive.

As I loaded all three children into the car, I noticed Walter's tenseness. I had no idea what was going on with him, and my anxiety was growing. Walter hung back as I secured the children into their car seats. I could feel him watching my every move. Hesitantly, I opened the passenger side door. As I lifted my leg to get in, I noticed that the inside of the car looked like it was the entrance to the bowels of hell. That hallucination was my intuition speaking to me again. I put my foot back down on the cement and stalled as long as I could.

"What are you waiting for? Get in the car," Walter commanded.

I slowly lowered myself into the seat. I made sure not to make eye contact with him as I buckled in. I looked back at the children, though. They seemed agitated as if they had the same sense of doom I did. I gave them a reassuring smile and turned forward.

Walter dropped into the driver's seat, shaking the whole car with his weight. He abruptly shifted the gear and proceeded to drive aggressively. I was confused about the whole situation; it just didn't make any sense. I just knew something bad was going to happen in that car.

At that point, I didn't know that Walter had seen the milk in the refrigerator. That is why I said, "If we are only going to the store for food, we don't have to. I got a ride today and already got some."

That statement is what Walter was waiting for. The entire trip was a mere ruse. He pulled over.

My confession pulled all of Walter's rage to his core, where it knotted into a tight ball. When it reached critical mass, the ball of rage exploded. Suddenly, the massive arm of a

250-pound man swung on me. It slammed my head back with such force that I could feel my brain jostle in my skull as it hit the hard headrest.

Stunned, I froze for a few seconds. I was in such shock that I didn't realize Walter was pounding fierce blows into my face. I could barely see him through the sparkles dancing in front of my eyes. By the time I snapped out of it, Walter had busted my lip wide open and nearly dislocated my nose. I flailed my hands wildly in an attempt to block the onslaught, but to no avail. There was no way that I, a petite woman, could fend off that giant brute of a man.

Walter took advantage of the fact that I was trapped in a confined space with no way to escape. This put a satisfied smirk on his face as he pummeled me.

Solomon and Hannah started screaming when they saw the blood streaming from my nose and lip. I tried to protect my face from Walter and comfort them at the same time. When I somehow managed to pop my head up long enough to look toward the back seat, all I saw was horror in the children's faces.

I knew what their horror was about. The children had also been on the receiving end of some of Walter's frustration. Because of that, they believed that they were next in line for a beating. I felt such shame and embarrassment. No child should see their mother being abused, but mostly, they shouldn't feel like they are endangered themselves. They were innocents who I should've shielded from brutality. After all, isn't that what we escaped the Congolese government for?

When Walter's wrath was satiated, he started driving us back home. Again, I dared not look at him directly, but I saw him clearly in my peripheral vision. He looked so proud of himself, like he took his manhood back.

I, on the other hand, cupped my hands to catch the blood. In no way did I want to anger Walter again by letting the blood drip on the upholstery.

That was the day Walter died to me. I was a widow living with a baneful corpse. This dead man looked like he was alive, but no human with a living heart could've done what he had just done to me. I made the shortsighted decision to keep up the pretense that everything was all right at home. I would pretend that the fantasy man I loved was still breathing, living somehow. That mindset would make it easier to fulfill my part of the marriage contract.

I knew people were going to ask me about my battered face. I had already made up my mind to lie about it. However, Hannah was ever-ready to innocently reveal the truth about what really happened. Of course, I would quickly quiet her down before the other person registered what she said. But that didn't matter because the truth was written all over my face in big, purple bruises.

I wanted to get help, but I was still a foreigner in an unfamiliar land. Walter had given me the impression that I had no rights because I wasn't a citizen and that the United States would support whatever traditions the Congolese culture had. Therefore, I felt like I was stuck. I figured the best I could do was give Walter proper respect and not go behind his back for help ever again.

But that didn't make my relationship with Walter any better. His abuse grew more malignant by the day. Plus, we still needed more food and money for our growing family. Someone suggested I try the Workforce, a recruiting company. I was willing to do anything to alleviate Walter's stress level and ward off any future beatings.

Workforce found me a job as a cashier at a teacher/student store that was about to close and just needed someone to help with the liquidation. After I started work, the assistant manager left, and I took over the position. Even though I knew the store was closing, the work ethic instilled by Daddy made me work hard, regardless. I started implementing ideas that I learned from working at Daddy's factory and increased the morale of the staff. The store actually started to make a profit. A shrewd investor bought it and was so pleased with my work, he promoted me to manager. I even earned a substantial bonus for my efforts.

Though I appeared naturally confident at work, it was a learned confidence. I had some deep insecurity that would occasionally rise up. This was the fruit of living with Walter. Being his wife had diminished my normal confidence level and made me question myself: Was I good enough? Did I deserve what Walter was doing to me? Since I chose Walter, could I even be counted on to make sound decisions?

I also saw that Walter was becoming extremely jealous of me. He had to take lowly positions, while I was moving up. In a sense, I was emasculating him. I was becoming his nemesis.

Because Walter was abusing me, I did whatever I could not to provoke him—especially when it came to my career. I made sure I didn't give the appearance of flaunting my position. In many ways, I became more submissive at home to offset the growing imbalance in our work lives.

My deference didn't make a difference, though. Walter's thirst for absolute control over me couldn't be quenched. He longed for the dominant position he would've had if we had stayed in Africa. There, he could deal with my random displays of independence however he wanted to. He would've had a tribal support system that would back him up no matter what he decided to do to me.

As a married woman in Africa, I was considered a second-class citizen when compared to my husband. If I had the audacity to act up there, Walter would've had the right to take me down as he saw fit.

But in America, Walter didn't have his tribe to bolster him, and he feared losing his grip on a westernized wife. Therefore, it was imperative that he made sure I didn't know that I had rights and opportunities in America that didn't exist for most women in African tribal societies.

Walter knew I'd naively trust what he said and constantly frightened me with the idea that I had no real rights in America—that life for me in America was going to be a replica of what life would've been for me in tribal Africa.

I was truly convinced that Walter was the only thing I could depend on in the States.

Chapter 12

$\mathscr{I}$ spent the next year taking beatings. But I was not the only one suffering. Walter was not only a tribal husband, but also a tribal father. Tribal men saw the children as property just like the wife and treated them as such, and discipline from a tribal father was usually severe. So, I took his method of disciplining them as part of his tribal ways.

As a consequence, patience was not a virtue Walter had mastered did he care nor to. Fortunately for Solomon, Walter's outward annoyance was more restrained. This was due to Solomon being the first-born male child and having special favor. In fact, in our home, Solomon outranked me in importance.

Of course, children will be children, and Solomon made occasional mistakes. Walter managed to somewhat tone down his wrath as he chastised Solomon, but he was still a virulently angry man by nature. Therefore, whatever real frustration he may have had toward Solomon still needed an outlet. So, he transferred the majority of his upset at Solomon to me. My little boy could only watch helplessly as I was beaten up, and he internalized the guilt of wrongly believing that he caused his father's violence.

However, there was something more disturbing—ominous, even—about Walter's interaction with Hannah. I could sense a strangeness when Walter was in the same room as her. He would appear calm on the surface, but the space around him would fill up with an uncanny electrical charge that I could actually feel. This electricity would consume all the air, making it heavy with a weird, somewhat frightening energy. But I just couldn't discern exactly what it was.

The eeriness grew more sinister as the days passed. For some unknown reason, Walter became much more violent with Hannah than Solomon. There were so many nights when I had to rescue Hannah, saving her from one beating or another.

Afterward, I'd usually end up in Hannah's bed, trying to take away her fears and stroking her to sleep. Every time I had to do that, I wondered why Walter took out so much of his rage on Hannah. I thought it was because she was so much bigger than the average child her age. Maybe that was why he felt so comfortable hitting her like an older kid. But I sensed there was more to it. I could see it in his eyes … this malice … this disdain toward his little girl.

I tried to keep all the children with me as much as I could, away from Walter. But I had to go to work, and he refused daycare, feeling it was an unnecessary expense. He promised no excessive discipline and reassured me that I could trust him with the children, and all would be well. I reluctantly agreed. However, every time I had to leave my babies with him, I felt ill, and for good reason.

After being out one day, I returned home. I hadn't even made it to the front door when Hannah came running toward me as if death was chasing her.

"Mommy! Mommy! He's going to kill me!" Hannah screamed. "Help me! Please!"

Hannah's words may have seemed advanced for her age, but she was being brought up in a home where her father constantly threatened to kill her mother. She was just repeating the same pleas I had made when Walter beat me.

Walter was storming behind Hannah. I instinctively threw myself between him and her. He attacked me with his gigantic shoe, and it felt like I was being hit with a brick. The shoe landed mostly on my torso because Walter had learned not to leave marks on my face for the world to see.

But my interference was damned. He was determined to get to Hannah; he wanted to finish delivering the pain that he thought she was due.

The only thing that made Walter hesitate was the fact that the neighbors were home. He didn't want an apartment complex full of witnesses calling the police.

"Get inside right now," Walter ordered as he sneered at the neighbors' windows.

"No, I can't go in there. Just give me Solomon and Abigail, and I'll be gone," I said.

"You do know that you have no legal rights here. I am the husband, and my word is the law. If you try to get help, they will side with me and give me the children."

There was no way I was going to let Walter have the children. That is the only reason I agreed to go into the apartment. I dared not look down at Hannah; I was so scared of what I'd see. I wish I had known better and been stronger for Hannah at that moment. But I was doing what my culture had trained me to do: ignore the sins of my husband.

As I walked Hannah back into the apartment, I could feel her tiny hand tightly holding mine. She was trembling. I took her to the bathroom to get away from Walter. The dim glow from the hazy light revealed that her head was severely swollen. Without a thought, I swooped her up and gathered the other children. My allegiance to cultural and religious traditions disappeared for the sake of my child.

I told Walter I was taking Hannah to the hospital. I expected him to argue, but he sat on the couch watching TV like he couldn't care less. That was because he was starting to believe himself to be invincible.

A good girlfriend met me at the hospital. As we sat in the emergency room, she looked at me knowingly.

"What happened?" she asked, though she already knew the answer.

I looked away. "Oh, it was nothing. Okay, well, it started out as nothing. You know how Walter gets. He was just disciplining her, and she tried to run away and fell. That's how she got hurt."

"Fell? Celine, you know something's not right about Walter. He's dangerous. Hannah is being stitched up because of him. You can tell me whatever you want, but I know the truth. He could've killed her, you know."

I wanted to tell my friend everything. But I didn't think it would help. I was still under the impression that the children and I had no rights. I was doing everything I could at that moment not to fall completely apart.

The nurses kept passing by, giving me accusatory looks. My friend subtly used her body as a shield to block their penetrating stares. However, she went on privately chastising me and said, "I know you want to make this marriage work. But you really have to open your eyes about who Walter really is. For the sake of the children."

But I already knew who Walter was. He was a bully. He was an abuser. He was the tyrannical ruler of my life. And he was the man I loved.

The physician came over to speak to me. Brusquely, he told me that Hannah had sustained blunt force injuries, and her entire body was covered with bruises—old and new. He also informed me that the authorities had been called because of suspected abuse.

When the police came, I thought about what Walter had said about me not having any rights. I couldn't risk him somehow getting sole custody of the children or them getting sent back to Africa to only become the "property" of his dysfunctional family. Although it appeared counterintuitive, I lied about what really happened. I did this to protect my children and to make sure that I would stay around.

But not all of my motivation was altruistic. Part of the reason I didn't tell the truth was because I was still in love with Walter. Indeed, I was truly soul-sick. I had an irrational mind that had somehow adapted to living an insane life.

There were rare times when I despised Walter. But most of the time, I made sympathetic excuses for him. It didn't even matter that he was a spiritually dead corpse to me. The animalistic rush he inspired kept me loving him. Unfortunately, that love was greater than my hate.

I lied about what happened to Hannah and refused to press charges regarding the beating Walter had given me. My family was referred to the Georgia Division of Family and Children Services and ordered into counseling. By this time, Walter was so smug that he refused to attend even one counseling session because he had gotten away with everything. He got to keep his property—his family—and do what he pleased.

Even in America, Walter's tribal mentality—with my help—was winning.

Chapter 13

$\mathcal{O}$ ne of Daddy's friends told him about a horrifying dream she had. She dreamed that one of his daughters had been killed. Daddy, obviously shaken up, asked which one. She said the light-skinned girl. But she wasn't the only one to have dreamed of my death; my aunt had the very same dream.

I was so young when I got involved with Walter and had nothing to compare our relationship to. That's why what I had with Walter just seemed normal. Cultural influences brainwashed me into believing what my place as a woman was in relation to a man. I was now a shadow of who I was back in Africa. I was hollowed out and filled with the terrible fear of losing custody of my children and a corrupt love for Walter.

My attachment to Walter was founded on the possibility that my "dead" husband would somehow resurrect and be the Prince Charming I craved.

Occasionally, I had signs of hope. Walter would be a regular husband. He wouldn't do anything spectacular; he would just do average things like take the family out to dinner. Those moments were enough to keep my hopes up. That is why I stayed with the dead man.

However, those moments wouldn't last too long.

I decided to go to my church for guidance and support. But the small church lacked training and resources to tackle the problem of domestic abuse. However, even if those things were available, the members were firmly entrenched in community norms. Certain things that were deemed unacceptable in America were totally acceptable in Congolese culture.

The Congolese pastors didn't want to deal with the abuse Walter was subjecting me to. They were more comfortable pretending it away. But I insisted on help. This forced them to offer me coded advice. It was subtly suggested that I hide from the public what was going on in my home. After all, the reputation of the husband had to be preserved. I was inevitably directed to the Bible and sent on my way. At least they didn't tell me to pour some oil over Walter's shoes and pillow and pray over them like they would've done in the Congo.

I went home and endured more of Walter's abuse. I was resigned to my sad life and started to let go of any idea of happiness. But God had other plans and sent some joy back into my life: Peter.

Peter was in town to attend the wedding of a mutual friend. So much had changed since I'd last seen him. When I laid eyes on Peter, I was astonished. He had grown into manhood quite well. Though he was not a behemoth like Walter, he still possessed all the positive attributes of masculinity. He had become a Harvard-educated scientist and had a nice-looking wife who he loved. He was so thrilled to see me that he made a beeline straight to me.

"Celine! How long has it been?" Peter said. His arms were wide open to give me a hug.

Walter kept his distance, watching to see if I would obey his no-contact rule with other men. I reluctantly stretched out my hand to shake Peter's. In no way did I want a beating that night over a simple hug.

"My sister, after so many years, you want me to shake your hand? Please, hug me!" Peter exclaimed.

Images of Walter's fists ran through my head. As Peter waited for his hug, my eyes went back to Walter, and I kept my hand up for a shake. Peter totally ignored the handshake and went in for the hug. My heart stopped. Walter had forbidden me to hug any man because he believed that was a prelude to me cheating. I wondered how much of a beating Peter's hug had earned me.

Peter and his wife, along with some other friends, managed to invite themselves over to my apartment. I tried to discourage the visit, but the group insisted. I was caught between two factions: friends that I wanted to see and the ogre I lived with. I sided with my friends even though I knew I'd be in trouble with Walter.

The next day, all the visitors showed up. Their gaiety somewhat brightened up the drab atmosphere in my apartment. However, even their light couldn't conquer the darkness of Walter's attitude.

Walter sat across from my friends with a strong-faced frown. He made sure he didn't say a single word. He was determined to make them feel unwelcome, uncomfortable, and intimidated. He succeeded. The visit that was supposed to be a long evening of friends reliving good times was cut short. My friends practically ran for the door, trying to escape an awesomely awkward situation.

I stood at the front door watching them as they hurried to their cars. I was so sad and embarrassed. Not only did I feel more isolated, but now they knew the truth about my marriage. I slowly shut the front door because I would have to answer to my dictator. I turned around and smiled at Walter, hoping that would appease him. But it didn't. I received my punishment for having the nerve to think I could be happy.

Afterward, for the rest of the night, I felt like I was living in a scary movie. In that movie, I was kidnapped by a psycho and thrown into a box. I could hear the voices of the police, and I was screaming out. The police would get closer and closer to the box but couldn't hear me. The police would then leave, taking all my hope with them.

In the box, the only things I had were God and an instinct to survive.

Chapter 14

$\mathscr{I}$ remember one day my sister came to visit. Her mouth dropped when she saw my lip. It was swollen to twice its normal size with raw skin blistering out of a huge split. The flesh tried its best to repair itself by leaving a painful, reddish-black, crusting scar.

Walter snidely said, "I hit Celine. So what? She is my wife, and I can do to her whatever I want. I can slit her throat right in front of you, and there is not a thing you or your family can do about it."

That scenario summed up my life at that point. Over the years, my family watched my deterioration from a distance. If they had known of the devilish animosity Walter held for Hannah, they would've taken all the children from me. Without that closely guarded information, my family simply made an unspoken agreement with me not to interfere with my marriage. That caused some estrangement and left me more tethered to Walter than ever before.

The time came for me to see my gynecologist, and I was told that I was pregnant for the fourth time. Unlike my three previous pregnancies, I was disappointed by the news. It wasn't because I didn't want the baby. I just couldn't justify bringing another innocent child into my world of mayhem. I wished I could pray the baby away, back to heaven where it would be safe. But I knew that was impossible.

My doctor looked at me gravely and said, "There is something else. You've contracted a venereal disease."

The world instantly went into a freeze frame. I couldn't process the fact that Walter had not only cheated on me, but also infected me. As I grappled with the news, I could feel the phantom of Mother's submissive shadow looming in the room, growing larger and darker. God knows I didn't want to be like her, but I did exactly what Mother would have done. I chose to downplay the diagnosis for the sake of my marriage. Once again, I turned against myself in favor of someone else. All I could do was go home and try to suffer through another day.

Seasons changed, but my festering resentment did not. It prevented me from fully connecting with the baby growing inside of me. True, I knew that being Walter's wife meant I'd have to live with whatever problems he brought me. However, he had endangered the health of our child because he felt entitled to not only a devoted wife, but also all the carnal pleasure any *other* woman would let him indulge in. How was it fair that he had such impunity? I wouldn't have had the same privilege if I had stepped out.

As the pregnancy drew on, I thought about Mother more. I came to realize that I had misjudged her. The reason she stayed with Daddy wasn't because she thought she was less than him. She stayed because she was more multifaceted than my limited impression of her. She was a woman who had managed to mentally and spiritually survive the sometimes brutal paternalistic culture she was born into. She sacrificed herself for the happiness of her children and did whatever it took to make sure they had a prosperous life. If that meant accepting Daddy's affairs, she was fine with that.

I could feel the harsh judgment I imposed on Mother leave me. As I lifted that horrendous guilt off her, somehow a very small bit of my projected guilt went with it. Though I was still trapped in my own situation, at that moment, I recovered some of the emotional freedom I had lost.

Once again, however, Walter sought to destroy any hope or happiness I had gained. I was eight months pregnant. At that time, Walter allowed one of my young nephews to live with us for a short time.

The precious load I was carrying in my belly caused my joints and muscles to fiercely ache. The pain was compounded by the sheer exhaustion of taking care of small children. To make life a little easier for myself, I'd sometimes microwave the children's food and milk.

One particular day, Walter caught me microwaving milk and found that to be egregious. He threw out a long string of heinous insults. I tried to focus on the children as I poured their milk. He thought I was discounting him and felt compelled to smack me for it. The sting of his hand against my flesh must've felt good to him because he ramped up the violence.

In a ridiculous fit of rage, Walter picked up a vacuum cleaner and swung it like a bat, slamming my side. I crashed to the floor but somehow made sure not to fall on my pregnant belly. I could feel the cracking of my wrists as they took the brunt force of my palms hitting the floor. I wept as the hose wand slipped off the hook and whipped my skin. I somehow staggered to my feet, deflecting Walter's assault in vain. At the same time, Walter pounded the vacuum cleaner into me without remorse or pity.

The beating happened so fast that my nephew barely had time to react. But when he did, he bravely stepped between Walter and me, risking his own safety. I took that opportunity and ran to the front door. My sweat-drenched hands fumbled with the knob as I kept looking back over my shoulder. Walter pushed my nephew out of the way. But before Walter could get to me, I bolted out and ran straight into the rock-hard chest of a neighbor who had heard the commotion.

The neighbor was a burly man who practically hurled me into the safety of his apartment. He was one of only a few people who weren't intimidated by Walter and actually tried to goad him into a fight as a means of distracting him from me. This flustered Walter because he was not used to having to defend himself against someone of his same size and strength.

My savior, the neighbor, eventually came inside and called the police. At first, I was relieved. But when the police arrived, I was afraid like before and didn't want to press charges. Unfortunately, the police had seen too many domestic violence victims and were used to my reaction. They took Walter in anyway and interviewed him with the hope that he would incriminate himself. Walter, being so prideful, gave them what they wanted when he told them, "I'm an African man, and if she doesn't do what I say, I will kill her."

Walter's threat earned him charges and some jail time. I truly had no idea that he would be detained.

Because it was the weekend, the courts were closed, so Walter's case wouldn't be heard by a judge until the next work week. To me, emotionally, it felt like the weekend that would never end because I knew Walter would stew in his wrath, and there would be payback. This was the situation I had been avoiding … the reason I didn't press charges before.

The next time I saw Walter, he was wearing an orange jumpsuit. He glared at me with those remorseless eyes, looking like my future executioner. Dread jumped into me as I could see death coming, so I lied to the judge. How silly of me. I was merely postponing my day of reckoning.

However, the judge was no fool and saw through my deceptive account of events. He looked into my eyes, like a stern father would to a wayward child. Then he said, "I know it is just a matter of time. This man will kill you. I don't want someone ever to blame *me* for releasing him to you."

The judge ordered a court assistant to make me sign a document which stated that because I refused to cooperate, the court could only put Walter on probation, mandate counseling, and reduce the sentence to a misdemeanor.

Of course, upon Walter's release, his self-satisfied reaction was to call my parents back in Africa and tell them that he was going to kill me. I lived in sheer terror after that, more than ever before. Walter exacerbated my fear by constantly reminding me that "*the next time*" I wouldn't be able to call the police.

That is why I dreaded the birth of my baby. I knew the hell it was coming into. I hoped God's mercy would allow the baby to stay within the questionably safe confines of my womb. But nature didn't take into consideration my circumstances, and the baby was born right on schedule.

I was almost afraid to look at her. I needed confirmation from the pediatric nurses that she was okay, that Walter's moral slip and physical abuse didn't harm her. The nurses assured me that the baby was fine. Then I was able to enjoy her, Sophia.

Sophia stoked my burgeoning desire to stand and fight.

Chapter 15

$\mathscr{A}$s I entered my thirties, a fierce stir of independence started whirling in me, causing an internal crisis. Parts of me were still determined to be a faithful and obedient wife, while other parts were breaking off their chains. I dared not share this awakening with Walter and had no one else to confide in due to Walter's isolation tactics. I just kept up my usual routine of working, taking care of the children, and being the recipient of Walter's evil.

I knew that ever since Walter's arrest, he ruminated about the humiliation he felt. As a result, he dealt with me more violently than ever before. It seemed as though I was being punched, kicked, stomped, or thrown into walls nearly every day. Oddly, I didn't mind so much because the more Walter was focused on hurting me, the less he preyed on Hannah. So, every slap to my face brought me some relief, knowing that Hannah was not being stalked, captured, and devoured by the walking dead that lived with us.

Counseling wasn't helping at all. Both the counselor and I were shocked at how unrepentant Walter was. Walter arrogantly recounted the hows and whys of abusing me. Sometimes a great smile would cross his face and a deep, haughty laugh would bellow out of his mouth as he told stories about punishments he had given.

But more disturbing was what he said about Hannah. His whole demeanor changed. He'd go from gleefully speaking about punching me in the face to gravely serious and sadistic, recalling the pleasure he had when hurting that little girl.

The temperature in the room would actually drop and the air would go completely still, totally quiet with only his voice resonating through it.

A look of horror and disbelief spanned the counselor's face when Walter spoke. He had never had a case where a man took such enjoyment in abusing his daughter so brutally. The counselor just couldn't reconcile in his mind the reasons for Walter's actions.

But I thought I may have had answers. The only two things that made "sense" were that Walter had less empathy for Hannah because she wasn't a male child and she was the only daughter whose birth he did not witness. Those excuses still weren't reasonable, but they were the only ones my mind could come up with.

That is when I knew I couldn't bring one more child into the world with the corpse. As soon as I could, I went to the clinic and got on birth control. However, Walter found out somehow. As usual, he erupted, shoving me about and screaming. Walter's refusal to let me use contraception was one of his most effective methods of control. He figured impregnating me would guarantee that I'd willingly stay trapped.

But it was too late; the medication was already in my system. I gave myself a metaphorical high-five because this was my first move toward freedom and victory against Walter.

Chapter 16

I was not always a true praying Christian. I went to church, studied the Bible, and prayed regularly. But mostly, I was just going through the motions of religion and not having a personal relationship with God.

That all changed when, after a crying bout, I had a dream. In it, I actually met God. He was so great in size that I could only see His feet, at which I immediately fell.

I said, "All the tears and pain. Father, where have you been?"

God stood me up and replied, "I have heard your cries. I'm with you." He went on to give my spirit further instructions that my conscious mind wasn't letting me hear.

In a half-asleep state, I opened my eyes, my vision engulfed in darkness. I could feel Walter's hot, dry skin pressed against mine. I moved away from him, repulsed.

I could hear Sophia sweetly puffing out tiny breaths in her sleep. I silently asked God that if it was really Him in my dream, could He confirm it through the laughter of my baby. Suddenly, Sophia let out the most glorious laugh, even though she was still slumbering. I wept. I knew from that moment on that God was with me. I was changed forever.

The next night Walter was again agitated. He figured it was somehow my fault and gave me a beating in the kitchen. I listened to the gentle voice of God telling me not to fight back because that would make the situation worse. God also told me to call Walter's counselor in the morning.

Morning came. I behaved as mellow as my acting skills would allow. But as soon as I got to work, I called the counselor and told him what was going on. He gave me the number to the Atlanta Council on Battered Women's Shelter. When I hung up with the counselor, I felt like I was ready to leave my marriage; however, as the day progressed, doubt descended upon me.

God understood my hardheadedness and worked through Walter's savagery. Walter ended up raping me that night. As he forcefully penetrated and ripped through my body, I knew *that* was God showing me that this was the best I could expect if I decided to stay.

When Walter's sexual violence was satisfied, he jumped back on top of me. Without any real provocation, he wrapped his massive hands around my neck. At first, I didn't fight back, believing that all he was going to do was rough me up a little and get off. However, that was not the case. He wanted me dead.

I tried to scream, but Walter choked off my air supply. I knew I had to fight back and grabbed Walter's wrists in a desperate attempt to make him stop.

Unfortunately, I looked into his eyes. What I saw was utter hatred staring back at me, just like that woman on that old television show had seen as her mother choked her.

Walter tightened his grip and came to a point where he didn't even see *me* anymore. He had traveled back in time, and he was now looking down at the alternating faces of his mother and step-mother. In Walter's mind, not only was he taking my life, but also the lives of the mother who abandoned him and the step-mother who abused the power she had over him.

As hard as I tried, I just couldn't break Walter's hold. A few seconds more … I would've been gone. God was indeed making sure I got the message.

Okay, God, you win. I'm leaving this madness behind. I promise.

Amazingly, a miracle happened. Something—God—made Walter stop. He loosened his grip and slowly lifted off me. He looked like he was in a daze as he stared down at me. Dumbfounded, he went to the bedroom to get ready for his night shift.

I went to the shower to wash Walter off me. Breaking down, I leaned into the shower's spray and cried. My tears were bittersweet for all the years I wasted with a fiend and because I was given another chance at life, perhaps my final chance.

Sleep eluded me that night as I prayed deeply about what to do. God reminded me that I had to leave, and this was a one-shot deal.

The dreary morning arrived. Walter was almost home from his night shift. He was minutes away. However, I still hadn't called the shelter; I was just too scared. But God's voice prompted me to do so. When I did, I felt some relief as I dialed. Finally, I would have some backup—perhaps some big, strong men who would hold Walter down if he decided to hurt me.

"Hello, my name is Celine," I said to the anonymous person on the other end of the line. "I'm leaving my husband. He beats me. When can you send someone over to get me?"

There was a slight moment of silence, and then the soft-spoken woman said, "I'm so sorry, ma'am. We cannot come to get you. You will have to leave on your own."

I nearly dropped the phone. *I had to leave Walter all by myself as if he was just going to let me walk out that door?*

The shelter worker gave me instructions. "Make sure when you leave, you take your children and whatever else is precious to you. Going back to retrieve those things will not be an option. In fact, when you leave, you may be in much danger."

I hung up the phone. I was totally numb. But as scary as it was, I was determined to follow through with my plan. I had to fight myself—the fearful part—and get on with it. If I didn't do that, I would've stayed with Walter until he put me in the ground.

Chapter 17

I frantically threw a few baby clothes into trash bags, hoping I could get out of the apartment before Walter came home. But I wasn't fast enough.

I heard Walter's key in the door's lock. I got rid of the evidence by quickly tossing the trash bags behind the couch.

Walter lumbered in. I was jittery, and he sensed something was amiss. "What's wrong with you? Why are you acting funny?" Walter interrogated.

I passed him a fake smile. "Wrong? Nothing is wrong? I'm just glad to see you."

Walter didn't believe my explanation. As I watched him fall into bed, I knew I had to come up with a cover story just in case he heard me bumping around, gathering the children's and my belongings.

I said, "Oh, by the way, I'm going to the grocery store, and I'll be getting the kids ready. Is that all right with you?"

A suspicious look came over Walter's face, but he was just too tired to argue. "Whatever," he said, closing his heavy lids.

I knew what I did next was a matter of life and death, and it was the most terrifying time of my life. Truth be told, all of my options, whether I stayed or left, were life-threatening.

However, God had put into me that it was too late to change my mind. I had to go. Stealthily, I gathered my hard-earned diplomas. I fought too hard for those, and there was no way I was leaving them behind for Walter to destroy in retribution.

The children curiously watched me. I didn't want to alarm or excite them to the point that they'd wake Walter, so I told them we were all playing a game. I made sure they knew their part of the game was to be quiet and not wake up their father.

Little by little, I took items out and placed them behind a dumpster. That way, Walter wouldn't see the bundled items just in case he woke up. Every time I went back inside, I could hear the bed squeak under Walter's weight or him grumble in his sleep. My heart never beat so fast.

I chose to leave some things behind, symbolic of my shared past with Walter. As I tiptoed through the apartment, I realized I was happy to let them go.

When I was finally done, I got the things from behind the dumpster and placed them in the second-hand car Walter and I just purchased. After I filled the trunk to full capacity, I went back inside to get the children.

"Where are we going?" Hannah asked.

"Just out," I said, keeping a watchful eye on the bedroom door.

As I went to pick up Sophia, Hannah ran toward the bedroom door. She shouted, "Bye-bye, Daddy!"

I was amazed for the briefest moment that, despite all Walter had done to Hannah, she still loved him enough to let him know when she was leaving. But that thought quickly switched to abject terror. I stood there paralyzed, waiting for the large, wild animal to rush out. I thought about what would happen when he noticed things were missing. That would've been the end of me. My poor babies would've had their mother murdered right in front of them. However, Walter stayed out. God surely must've silenced Hannah's voice to Walter's ears.

All of a sudden, I heard God telling me to get out of the apartment as fast as I could. I grabbed Sophia and Abigail up in my arms and ran out with Solomon and

Hannah. It was difficult running to the car with four kids, but I made it. I hastily pushed Hannah and Solomon into the car and halfway buckled the younger two into their car seats.

The noisy car started up with me cursing it. All the while I kept looking back toward the apartment. I almost backed into another car and had to brake abruptly. I had some trouble shifting the grinding gear into drive, but when I did, I peeled out.

God took over, and I drove to the shelter in a trance. As soon as I got there, I grabbed my kids and ran for dear life into the building. Waiting for me were serious yet concerned women who ushered me in. Some of them stood guard at the door as someone led me to the front desk for initial processing.

As I was giving them my information, my eyes glazed over, and I became lightheaded. The room started spinning as I came to the awful realization of what I had just done. I practically tossed Sophia into the arms of a caseworker, just as my legs buckled beneath me. Exhaustion and terrified shock took over. I fainted, becoming a pile of skin and bones on the floor.

The staff didn't panic, having dealt with this same situation before with other abused women. They followed a treatment protocol and placed me in a room to recuperate.

While I slept, Walter had become aware of what I had done. He flew into an inhuman state that went far beyond rage. He ripped, punched, and tore up the apartment as if it was me. But all that did was magnify his blind bloodlust.

Walter called my brother to see if he knew where I was. My brother was very aware of Walter's history of mayhem and started to cry. He believed that I'd never had enough bravery to leave Walter. Therefore, if I was missing, Walter was playing a mind game with him and surely must've killed me. Convinced I was dead, my brother called my pastor and the police and told them to go to the apartment to retrieve my body and arrest Walter.

But by the time the police arrived, it was too late. Walter had already stormed out of the apartment. He intended to bring me back to torture and kill me. His search took him to places familiar to me like my job, church, and friends' homes. He accosted everyone who had even the slightest contact with me, verbally and physically assaulting them to learn my whereabouts.

They said they had no clue where I was, and that was the truth. I had firsthand knowledge of Walter's predatory nature. Like an animal, he could smell a lie emanating from someone's skin. Therefore, I was not willing to risk the possibility of a friend or family member giving up my location under threat. That is why I was so careful not to divulge my plans to anyone, the only exception being Walter's counselor.

Walter continued his maniacal search for the children and me. Meanwhile, I hid out. As soon as I started to relax, a caseworker came in. She said they had just received word that Walter knew where I was and was threatening not only me, but also any person who tried to block him from taking revenge. His only objective was to kill me. He was resolute.

The shelter took this threat seriously and tried to protect us as best they could. Unfortunately, the shelter didn't have enough permanent room for us. But they found another shelter with enough space in Louisiana. I didn't care where we had to go and was thankful that they arranged everything for us to travel.

I was in a total state of flux, reeling from my abrupt departure from Walter. I just wanted a chance to collect my thoughts, to slow down enough to just *breathe*. I so dearly wanted a timeout. But that wasn't going to happen. I had to take control of my life for a change. I had given so much control to Walter—how could I possibly be expected to master myself?

And then I looked at my children. They were standing there so solemn, their faces filled with uncertainty. Something inside of me spoke. It told me taking charge of my destiny wasn't for me; it was for them. I had to stop obsessing about my perceived faults and self-pity and put all my focus on them. I didn't have to have all the answers. I only had to trust myself enough to make a good choice, and that choice was traveling to Louisiana to face more unknowns.

After a long bus trip paid for by the shelter, we ended up in Lafayette, Louisiana. Our new home was a homeless shelter called the Faith House. We settled in and began the process of rebuilding our lives.

It was not surprising to me that the three older children bore deep scars. After all, they were old enough to understand and remember what had happened to them. But it had escaped my awareness that an infant as young as Sophia was traumatized, too.

I learned this one day when a friendly maintenance man came into our room. He was a rugged black man who very much resembled Walter. He immediately caught Sophia's attention. Sophia, who had been playing on the floor, started screaming as the maintenance man walked toward her. She had just learned to crawl and quickly got on her knees. She wriggled away as fast as she could and made it to a wall. She kept looking back at the maintenance man who was trying to soothe her with kind words. But all she saw was Walter's face. Sophia turned back toward the wall and basically tried to claw through it to get away.

I picked Sophia up as she bucked and kicked against me. She wasn't just crying; she was wailing with anguish. I swaddled her to calm her down. The maintenance man looked at me; he was totally perplexed.

"I'm so sorry. I didn't want to scare her like that," the confused man said.

"It isn't your fault. You just remind her of someone," I answered.

He gave me an understanding nod. "I won't be coming back. I'll send someone else if you need something."

It took quite some time, but when Sophia did calm down, she went to sleep for hours and hours. As I watched her, I thought about my children's futures. I wanted to see them take from their childhoods lessons that would help them become happy, well-adjusted human beings. But the way things were going, it looked like the mental delirium caused by abuse would be their only legacy.

Chapter 18

I started divorce proceedings and was lucky that face-to-face interaction with Walter wasn't necessary. There would be days when it seemed like all I did was write my signature on never-ending sheets of legal documents. But I didn't mind because my pen and those pieces of paper were like a master key and many jail cell locks. Every scribble helped put an end to my captivity.

However, church doctrine and my upbringing whispered to me. They relentlessly reminded me that God hated divorce and that I was wrong for leaving Walter. The guilt was all-consuming at times.

But I couldn't help but think that if God hated divorce, why didn't He just take Walter? Just kill him. After all, God saw how he treated me, despite my devotion. God could've at least rendered me a little bit of justice. But the Holy Spirit rebuked me, and I was forced to repent for wishing death on my enemy.

The Holy Spirit started taking down walls that I'd built around my life, walls that prevented God's goodness from coming in. The Spirit didn't bulldoze the walls right away, though. God's plan was to be brought about in a slow, methodical way, taking down one painful brick at a time. This was necessary to clear out my internal chaos.

God was mainly in the process of cutting any attachments I had with Walter. That is why He put me in that strange city where I didn't know anyone except my kids. He wanted me to lean on Him and not share His glory with any man—including Daddy.

Coincidentally and with reluctance, Daddy decided to visit me just when my rickety car gave out. I couldn't afford another one and could see that Daddy was once again ashamed of the ignoble condition I was in. My brother suggested that Daddy buy me another car. Daddy's response was that he didn't come to deal with my problems, and he left without offering me any help.

I knew Daddy was tired—tired of my endless drama with Walter, tired of being disappointed by my poverty, and most of all, tired of struggling with my pain that he couldn't fix. Despite Daddy's cold shoulder, I didn't have any resentment toward him because I felt that his attitude was part of a much bigger plan.

God, however, did come to my rescue. His glory worked through a neighbor, Big Bob, who graciously let me use his truck. Big Bob was a large, blue-collar man who was never in danger of being invited to any sort of fancy soiree. His truck was his mechanical twin—a jalopy that reeked of stale cigarette smoke and was filled with crushed, empty beer bottles. But Big Bob's truck was like a limousine to me.

Big Bob's unpretentious attitude and selfless care made him royal in my eyes. Looking back, it's funny how guardian angels take form. And Big Bob wasn't the only angel in Lafayette.

At the shelter, I met Miss Stephanie. She showed me the ropes and never looked down on me. She made me feel as though I was her equal, even though I was at the beginning of my recovery. This extraordinary lady showed me how to put my children in the Big Brothers Big Sisters program, where they could do fun activities and make friends. She even taught me how to get psychological counseling, in particular when the demon of depression first started making itself known.

The United Way was another boon, providing donated clothing trailers with decent attire. Those trailers were filled with clothes from women who probably had no idea how those items helped women like me. Those clothes raised my self-esteem and increased my faith in humanity. People were good. The only problem was that I couldn't see that goodness in myself yet.

Though I made progress, it was not as quick or painless as I'd wished. I still had feared that Walter would show up and slit my throat. On top of that, I felt like the overwhelming sense of anxiety was going to keep me submerged in pain. But I just suppressed what I was feeling so that I could function enough to take care of my children. I actually found some peace in the fact that Solomon and Abigail had made some headway in their emotional recovery.

Even Hannah managed to find some solace by playing "second mommy" to her siblings. During that erratic time, watching over her brother and sisters was the only thing that brought a smile to Hannah's face. However, she would sometimes be hypervigilant and too protective of them. Just like me, she was waiting for Walter to show up to kill us all. This wasn't only evident at home, but at the school as well.

Hannah's teacher called me in for a conference. I learned Hannah had been acting out in class. The teacher assumed it was out of embarrassment over a field trip Hannah had missed because I didn't have the money for it. Hannah had to spend the day being babysat in a lower grade class while her friends enjoyed the day out. I admitted to the teacher my financial predicament and some of Hannah's abusive past.

However, I knew there was much more going on with Hannah. Something was bothering her. But I was barely holding myself together and just couldn't face any more heartache. So, I decided the best course of action would be not to discuss the past with Hannah, hoping that somehow the horror of her memories would fade away.

Walter certainly had given Hannah and me an awful education. What we learned was that a man's "love" comes with a stipulation. You have to sacrifice something you *don't* want to give up.

The thing you'll be forced to sacrifice is your expectation of being loved unconditionally. The more you fight that reality, the more sacrifice you'll be forced to make to obtain his so-called love. The sad part is that if the man takes the sacrifice, he automatically *has* to love you conditionally. And that is really no love at all.

Chapter 19

Guilt is a destroyer, an eater of the soul. It makes you accept things and people into your life that you shouldn't.

The year was 1998. I had made some progress, yet constant guilt made me ruminate about all the mistakes I had made in my life. I wrecked my relationship with Daddy, chose a monster for a husband, and let my children witness and suffer through abuse. I most certainly thought I deserved all the difficulty that I was experiencing and then some.

The children and I had left the shelter a year prior and moved into a house with three other adults, including a friend named Peggy. But eventually, the house was sold. We had tremendous difficulty finding another one that would accept all of us. Consequently, we had to separate, but that allowed me to find a place of my own in Broussard. The next obstacle was figuring out how I was going to move. I went straight to church and prayed. God answered before I got up from the pew.

A stranger tapped me on my back and passed me a note. It said that God knew all my needs and would see me through. It was such a timely message that I could do nothing but cry. After the service, the stranger was waiting for me in the parking lot. She was a kind, middle-aged woman named Ms. Margaret.

Ms. Margaret's tender demeanor reminded me of how much I missed Mother and had longed for the comfort of her touch. Ms. Margaret said, "I am a minister, and I help young women who are experiencing a difficult time. Tell me, do you have a specific need that my ministry could help you with?"

"I need someone to help me move," I responded without hesitation.

Sure enough, Ms. Margaret had a son who owned a truck. His name was Samuel, and he agreed to help me. I must admit that when I first saw him, I was shook. I wasn't expecting him to be so handsome. He had a dashing smile that would make any woman forget about her pain. Not only that, but Samuel seemed to be one of the nicest, most kind people in the world. That answered prayer about moving came with a fringe benefit.

The evening was falling when Samuel arrived. I answered the door and was greeted by his silhouette, framed by the setting sun. If my intuition had been awake, Samuel's shadowed appearance would've looked more like the horror he really was. I invited Samuel to come in as I introduced him to Peggy. She was acting as chaperone and easing my nervousness.

I acted like a giggly schoolgirl as Samuel walked in. He didn't waste any time and immediately started packing boxes and pushing heavy furniture around. I watched him and was spellbound by his Adonis-like frame and masculinity.

Peggy didn't have the same reaction toward Samuel and was immediately put off. Something about him definitely raised her hackles. Samuel tried to charm her with witty banter, but Peggy wasn't having it. The whole time Samuel was there, Peggy sneered at him and shook her head at me as I gazed longingly at him.

After Samuel put the last box into the truck, he turned to me. He said, "A beautiful woman like you shouldn't be alone. I'd love to spend some more time with you, if that's okay."

It had been such a long time since anyone said I was beautiful. I could hardly believe a young and attractive man would even look at a single mom who was not too far removed from a shelter. I thought if I didn't take him up on his offer, I might not ever get another chance at romance. I quickly said, "Yes."

My relationship with Samuel progressed quickly. He seemed like a dream come true. He acted like a God-fearing man; in fact, he was a worship leader at his mother's church. I even officially joined the congregation with his encouragement. He was also always there whenever I needed some manly chore done around my house.

But sexual temptation arrived, and I succumbed. I was shocked and ashamed at what I'd done. I was disappointed that I let myself fall into sin like I had done with Walter before our marriage. I felt like a hypocrite going to worship service and interacting with Ms. Margaret as if I wasn't fornicating with her son.

I would take a seat and watch Samuel lead worship service, praising God without a care in the world. It was amazing that he could compartmentalize sex and God. This disturbed me so much that I was compelled to bring out a Bible to show him scriptures that proved sex outside marriage was wrong. Samuel responded by throwing the Bible into the trash. That's when I knew I was in trouble.

To assuage my guilt, I confessed to Ms. Margaret. She looked at me matter-of-factly and said, "You were taken advantage of because you're a single mother, vulnerable. You're not the only one. Samuel is going out with several girls in this church."

I was flabbergasted. "Why do you keep him in the church and let him lead worship services?" I said as my hands gestured displeasure.

"Because he needs to be in the house of the Lord. One day the Holy Spirit is going to touch him and set him free. Can you imagine how terrible he'd be if he wasn't in church?"

I just slumped down in my chair. I couldn't believe Ms. Margaret was protecting Samuel.

"Celine, Samuel is old enough to get married. Haven't you asked yourself why he hasn't introduced you to the church as his woman?" Ms. Margaret said with an accusatory tone.

I knew I'd get no understanding from Ms. Margaret, who was letting her son use the church as his personal nightclub. I gathered my things and vowed that I would end it with Samuel. I silently asked God to set me free as I walked to my car. But as I was driving home, guilt spoke to me. I felt dirty, contaminated by Samuel's filth.

When I arrived home, I ran to the shower and turned the water to an extremely hot temperature. I let it run and went to the kitchen for olive oil. I was going to perform an exorcism. I got into the shower and poured the entire contents of the olive oil on my head, crying and begging for God's intervention. That oil represented the Holy Spirit and God's holiness flowing from my head to my feet. As my hands slipped over my body, I felt as though I was released from the bondage of fornication.

But the oil had gotten into my eyes and left me nearly blind for two days. Though my physical eyesight was blurred and I had excruciating pain, my spiritual eye was opened. God was with me once again.

Samuel wasn't done with me, though. He started playing head games when he realized I was no longer interested in him. He decided to use my jealousy against me. During Sunday services, Samuel would make sure I saw him sitting extra close to other female congregants or be obscenely flirtatious with them. It worked. My emotional immaturity made me feel ugly and rejected. I knew the best course of action would be for me to find a new church.

However, in an effort to lead me back into a promiscuous lifestyle, Samuel showed up at my door late one night. I was still weak for him and let him in against my better judgment.

The visit started out innocently enough but quickly devolved. Samuel demanded sex that I didn't want to give.

I asked him to leave, using my sleeping children as an excuse. But he wouldn't be deterred and brutally raped me. I wanted to scream from the pain, but my children were only a few feet away in the other room. Hence, I endured the rape like a patient receiving surgery without anesthesia.

A few days later, one of Samuel's scorned church "girlfriends" told me about his extensive criminal record. He was convicted of various sex crimes, including rape. I realized this is what guilt brought to me. Though I was thankful my girls were spared, I felt like I was punched in the soul with the full realization that if God had not intervened, they would've been next.

Guilt is what made me seek out validation from just about anybody to prove that I wasn't as bad as I thought I was. It was obvious that I had to purge myself of my negative mindset if I ever expected to move forward. However, instead of working through the tremendous pain, I pushed it down even further.

This irrational decision is what made it possible for guilt and its ugly consequences to show up in my future, over and over again.

Chapter 20

*I*n 2001, I moved to Dallas at the behest of my brother. Though the move wasn't an easy one, my fledgling confidence allowed me to get a decent home, find a great church family, and secure a job at Texas Instruments.

But my past found yet another way to hold me back. I had come to the United States with a visitor's visa that was later converted to asylum status due to Walter's military desertion. My divorce forced me into an immigration battle because Watler was the reason for my asylum. The United States declared that I wasn't a person of interest to the Congolese government and sent a notification that they would start deportation proceedings against me.

There was no way I was going back to the paternalistic oppression of the Congo and its vengeance waiting for me. Moreover, I couldn't stomach the idea of Walter getting sole custody of the children if I was sent back. I sought out legal help, but it seemed almost all Texas attorneys had no sympathy or patience for the plights of single, poor women.

I was eventually referred to an attorney. He charged me a $1500 retaining fee, money I could scarcely afford. But I managed to scrape up a portion of the money, believing that man would save me. As the attorney counted the money, he promised to meet me in Houston for my interview with immigration.

The morning of the interview, I rose before the sun just to make sure I got to Houston before my interview time. I arrived at the courthouse with plenty of time to spare and used the extra hour to settle my nerves. However, when my time came up, my attorney still had not arrived. The judge asked me if I wanted to reschedule and was kind enough to call my attorney.

To my surprise, the devious attorney had simply decided not to come. The judge was sympathetic to my plight and let me plead my case right then and there. I broke down as I spoke about the torture that most likely awaited me in the Congo. Afterward, the judge told me that I would get a response to my case within thirty days.

I went back to Dallas with hope and anger at the no-show attorney. I called him multiple times, but he never picked up. I found out later that he was disbarred for fraudulent activity. Not only did I lose my money, but my case was denied by immigration.

However, God was watching out for me. An attorney I had been working with in Louisiana had a connection to a human rights attorney in Dallas, Elise Ealy. I met with Elise, a passionate woman, who agreed to work for me *pro bono*. She enthusiastically pleaded my case; however, it was concluded not to be a human rights case, since Mobutu was no longer in power and I wasn't Walter's wife.

Meanwhile, a child psychologist was assigned to my case. The psychologist determined that the children were enduring the trauma of not knowing if I'd be able to stay in the United States and if they'd be sent to Walter.

Counsel posted a question that gave insight to the court. What if Walter decided to go back to Africa with the children? The children would have terrible health care and possibly reduced educational opportunities. The daughters would suffer at the hands of misogynists, and the son would be trained to subjugate women.

After a few weeks, Elise had prepared another strong case for me. Being a woman enabled her to totally empathize with the awful reality of women in the Congo. This made her even more battle-ready as she stood with me before another judge. Miraculously, the attorney for the immigration didn't even ask us questions; everything was simply settled in my favor.

The judge did have some questions, though. He asked, "What do you want today?"

"To watch my children grow up in this country and pursue the American Dream," I answered, trembling.

"What kind of income do you see yourself making in ten years?"

"I'll make $100,000 a year," I blurted out. At the time, I thought I was just a crazy dreamer. I didn't realize God was speaking through me.

I thanked Elise and left the court feeling like a weighted vest had been taken off me. I went home and did something I had not done in a while; I relaxed.

Time went on, and my family was making progress. The children were in school, and I worked, albeit very hard. It seemed like I had closed the door on my past and was walking into my future.

However, one day, the phone rang. I looked at the Caller ID and didn't recognize the number. I figured it was one of my fellow church members or just a wrong number. I answered nonchalantly.

An awful voice was on the other end of the line. It was Walter. I felt as though I had been tossed into a frozen lake. All the fear and helplessness reawakened in me.

Walter bragged about how he could find me anywhere and made veiled threats about coming to my home and harming me.

I had two choices. I could submit to the corpse like I had done during our marriage or stand up for myself. I chose the latter.

My back straightened, and my lungs filled with air. With bass in my voice, I said, "You can't and won't do anything to me. If you dare come here, I will call the police and make sure you go to jail."

I could hear Walter take in a shocked breath, sounding almost like a woman. Before he could think of another impotent threat, I hung up on him. I was proud for a moment, but then I thought, *What have I done? He's surely going to come for me.* But God calmed me down and assured me I was safe.

A self-congratulatory smile came over my face. I had stood up to the beast and caged him for a change.

Chapter 21

$\mathcal{I}$ had been living in Dallas for a while and was tired of renting. After much consideration, I decided to become a homeowner. God directed me to a wonderful realtor and broker named Jane Lin.

My trepidation made me want to ease into the process, so I called Jane's office on a rainy Sunday, preferring to speak to a machine. But Jane's imposing voice greeted me instead. Startled, I rambled a bit. Jane took control, as she was all business, and told me to come over straight away.

I arrived at the office expecting to see a large, boxy woman to match the voice I had heard on the phone. But the commanding presence sitting behind the desk was a diminutive Chinese lady. It took a moment for me to reconcile Jane's petite frame with her authoritative phone voice. The best way for me to hide my surprise was to go right into a long-winded monologue about how I wanted to buy a house.

Jane just sat there, nodding as if she was trying to get me to get to the point. When I finally stopped talking, she started asking me guided questions to go beyond the superficial reasons I wanted a house and find out my true intentions. She had a way about her that made me feel safe enough to let some of my discontent spill out.

I told Jane about wanting to be more than what I was—a customer service representative, basically surviving in someone else's home. Though I was practically broke, I knew that someday my children and I would have more and *be more*, and a home of our own was a symbol of that.

Jane thought for a moment and said, "I'm not going to help you buy your house. Instead, you'll buy your house, on your own, as a realtor."

I sat there dumbfounded as Jane slid papers over to me. They stated that I was to be my own realtor and contained information about the required classes for me to go through.

My thought about Jane was that she was crazy. Even though I hated my job and was barely scraping by, at least I was getting a weekly paycheck. How did Jane think I was going to pay for the classes? Did she really think I could risk living off commissions? Basically, she was telling me that if I didn't sell, the kids and I wouldn't eat.

But money wasn't my only concern. My mental state wasn't the best. I was fluctuating between self-confidence and anxiety attacks. I couldn't see how I could steady myself long enough to convince others to invest hundreds of thousands, maybe millions, in a property.

Jane's offer was another crossroad in my life, and I had to decide who I was going to be. I could've stayed at Southwestern Bell, where I was working at the time. However, I had spoken with other women who had been employed there for years. They were absolutely miserable. The very thought of ending up like them terrified me.

If I wanted a different life, I had to be radical. Fear told me I would fail, but God's counsel told me to leap and He'd catch me. Needless to say, I took Jane up on her offer and started my unexpected real estate career.

Becoming a realtor wasn't easy. Since I was the sole provider for my children and worked during the week at Southwestern Bell, I could only take classes on the weekends. Though I struggled through some of the coursework, I became more and more convinced that real estate was my calling. I was happy and felt like I was accomplishing something great.

However, I had a detractor. A particular male instructor seemed to have it out for me. One day, he was asking the students about their backgrounds. When my turn came, I was so excited to tell my story about immigrating to America and overcoming adversity. He didn't seem impressed and acted like there was something about me that annoyed him.

The instructor interrupted with an invasive question. He sneered, "Anyway, how much money do you have saved up?"

"Well … um … I'm a single mother of four. Whatever money I get has to be used immediately for living expenses," I said meekly.

With a cruel smirk, the instructor said, "You should have at least six months' worth of living expenses saved up. That's why people like you won't make it. You're wasting your time."

The instructor went back to teaching the class only seconds after arrogantly trying to make an example out of me. I hunched over, feeling so little and embarrassed as the other students' eyes landed on me with pity.

But something rose in my soul and told me to sit up straight. My combative spirit *silently* entered a bet with the instructor. It bet him that I wouldn't be a statistic and would prove him wrong. The instructor obviously didn't know the God that I served.

I finished my classes, but not without some sacrifice. As the sole provider, I had no other person to help pay for the classes. As a result, there was barely any extra money left in the family budget, and my children's needs were put on hold many times. But it was necessary to get us all to a better place.

It also didn't help that I got fired from Southwestern Bell. This happened because I was not rebutting and trying to sell bigger packages to customers. The actual call that led to my firing was from an elderly woman complaining about how high her bill was due to a new plan. I knew she was on social security and arranged for her to have her old, cheaper plan back. The higher-ups were listening in on the conversation and didn't like that at all. But God was speaking to me, and He said that helping her was the right thing to do.

So, there I was, subsisting on the tiny bit of unemployment that I had to fight Southwestern Bell for, and I still wasn't making any realtor commissions. Many days, I would get to work and wonder how I would transport clients to see houses because I didn't have enough gas money. Sometimes, it got so bad that I thought my instructor would win the bet … that maybe he was right.

Fortunately, Jane and I made a secret arrangement where she'd pay me $50 per week to clean the bathrooms. It provided gas money but still wasn't enough.

A moment of desperation made me get an application to work at another call center. I was fully ready to end the folly of my real estate dream. I put the pen on the paper but couldn't move it to write a single letter. Suddenly, I heard the soft voice of God ask, "Why don't you trust me?"

I dropped the pen and cried. I never filled out the application. I decided to trust God, and I'm glad I did because He knew that I'd become one of Dallas's most successful brokers in real estate one day. All I had to do was gird myself with faith and make it through the scary, lean times.

God wasn't the only father showing his love for me at that time. I received a surprise phone call from Daddy. The Holy Spirit compelled him to call and apologize for his past behavior and how it impacted the choices I'd made. Daddy humbly asked for my forgiveness, and I gave it to him. Daddy's remorse let me know that I was still special to him. No longer would I have to use other men's "affection" as a substitute for his.

Though I was grateful for the apology, I had matured enough to know that I still had deep wounds to heal. Daddy's apology was just one of many developments that would lead me to my ultimate metamorphosis. But how quickly and by what means my restoration would come was strictly up to me.

he Bible said I couldn't serve two masters; I would hate one and love the other. I knew those words were referring to money and God and about declaring which one I'd trust. But I must admit that money won my allegiance many times. See, sometimes I treated my faith as a luxury good, only to be enjoyed when my choices weren't rooted in survival. I'm not talking about personal survival; I'm talking about the survival of my family. That's why, though I didn't love money, for my family, I desperately grasped for it.

After I obtained my realtor's license, commissions didn't immediately flow in. Selling was hard, and profits from the few sales I managed to make, were instantly devoured by household bills and feeding four growing children.

I had to spend an inordinate amount of time at work to make whatever money I could. This left my unsupervised two older children vulnerable to unsavory influences. If I wasn't so busy, I would've seen the insidious changes taking hold of Solomon and Hannah.

Solomon, though still an innocent child in many respects, had reached the age of rebellion. He was testing his burgeoning manhood and needed a father figure to guide his way. Unfortunately, the only male influence Solomon could remember was Walter—that creature—and even he wasn't in Solomon's life. This left Solomon searching for any male influence and connection. That is how a gang recruited him.

I had no clue about Solomon's involvement with the gang. Solomon made his relationship with the boys appear innocent. Little did I know that he was actually in the process of being initiated into a life of crime.

Then there was Hannah, who was just eleven years old at the time. Trouble found her through a thirteen-year-old prostitute in the neighborhood. The salacious girl's name was Scarlet.

Scarlet was like the driver of a red-hot sports car with Hannah riding shotgun, her hand waving blithely in the wind. Just as Scarlet seduced clients, she knew how to beguile Hannah. Hannah's clouded vision wouldn't allow her to see Scarlet as the lowly child prostitute she was. Instead, Hannah saw Scarlet as a vivacious girl with whom she could trade beauty tips, exchange laughs, and share secrets.

When Hannah asked Scarlet about her activities, Scarlet glossed over the deviant aspects and focused on the money. Scarlet often made a show of all the clothes, purses, and gadgets she was able to buy. Hannah was impressed and jealous, wishing she had enough cash to buy trinkets and eat junk food at the food court like any other girl.

However, our family always seemed to be in a financial bind. There were times when we still relied on donations, and income for entertainment was unheard of. Though Hannah was a motherly type, she was also just a typical American girl and had some resentment that she couldn't partake in all the preteen rituals.

Hannah could only live the "dream teen" life vicariously through Scarlet. Scarlet knew this and enticed Hannah with a little bit of her profits, so that she'd be able to control her. Hannah didn't think about where the money came from; she only cared that she was living richly through Scarlet.

The more money Hannah got from Scarlet, the more she wanted to be with her, and at some point, Hannah's interest in Scarlet went past the material benefits. Hannah actually grew to worship the enchanting illusion Scarlet conjured up. To Hannah, Scarlet not only had wealth, but Scarlet was also in total control of her own life; Scarlet misled Hannah to think that. Therefore, Hannah never knew how sad and scared Scarlet really was.

Another reason Hannah had fallen under Scarlet's influence was that they shared a spiritual tie formed through tragedy. Both of these lonely girls had experienced abuse at the hands of someone who was supposed to love them. Hannah was tortured by her father and Scarlet was pimped by her uncles. The girls were struggling with their spiritual sicknesses in their own ways, but money was a remedy for both of them.

To the girls, money was more than a tool to buy stuff. It was the god that seemed to take away their pain, even though the effect was temporary. The girls preferred to feel good for a moment rather than feel anguish all the time.

Eventually, I did see the disturbing nature of Scarlet and Hannah's relationship and forbade Hannah from seeing Scarlet again. But just as much as I was determined to see Walter so many years earlier, Hannah was determined to keep seeing Scarlet.

Hannah ran away from home with Scarlet; it was like they evaporated into thin air. Hannah just wanted to be carefree like a regular kid and running away was her attempt to save herself. Hannah was dying inside and had to get away from her pain, embarrassing poverty, and even me. To Hannah, the home was only walls and space filled with despair.

I didn't care about Hannah's motivation. I just wanted my child back. I went to the police, mistakenly believing that my sweet Hannah would be a priority. But they were blasé about her case. I didn't know why, whether it was just so common for kids to run away or if it was due to my station in life.

Regardless, law enforcement was casual about Hannah and simply designated her as a mere runaway.

If I had more money, none of this would've happened, I thought. Instead of trusting God, desperation made me wish for that other master.

Chapter 23

I thought I'd known terror when I was married to Walter. However, I didn't truly experience it until Hannah's disappearance. Racked with torment, I couldn't eat, sleep, or even breathe as I prayed for my baby to come home.

But one day, there was a break in Hannah's case. Investigators found paperwork hidden inside Hannah's school locker. Flipping through its pages, they realized it was detailed instructions from Scarlet's pimps telling Hannah how to run away and assume another identity. When the investigators informed me of what they'd found, I knew I'd never see my precious daughter again. There was nothing left to do except grieve the loss of her.

However, Hannah must've wanted to be found because she was discovered idly standing on the street in full view of the truant officers who brought her in. Fortunately, Scarlet wasn't with Hannah. Otherwise, she would've tipped Hannah off, and the girls would've disappeared, possibly forever.

Hannah got into a police cruiser as ordered, but she kept nervously looking out the window. The officers noticed Hannah's fidgety behavior and figured she was not acting alone. They started to interrogate Hannah about what was really going on, but she remained tight-lipped.

Meanwhile, I was in a disconnected state and trying to manage my other children. I noticed that Solomon was becoming disruptive as he got more involved with that roguish group of boys. Solomon's and Hannah's antics were driving me toward a nervous breakdown. I was using every emotional resource I had to stay sane for my two younger children.

Prayer was the only comfort I could rely on, and I was deep in it when the phone rang. With sluggish steps, I made my way across the room and answered.

"Hello," I said with a heavy heart.

"Celine, some truant officers found Hannah and brought her to the station," said the investigator.

I was so overwhelmed, I nearly fainted and said, "Praise be to God!"

"But there's a problem. Hannah refuses to talk. Maybe you can talk some sense into her."

I hung up the phone and as fast as I could get there, I was at the police department. However, I was shocked by Hannah's condition. Her body looked frail and thin, a far cry from the strong, robust girl I knew her to be. I stared into her vacant eyes as I knelt by her side and took her into my arms.

"Momma, I can't tell them what happened," said Hannah, quavering. "Scarlet's family said they'd hurt you if I told on them."

I took Hannah's tear-streaked face into my hands. "You've got to tell them everything. Those men can't go around helping girls run away."

"I'm not going to talk. I'm just not."

The investigators and I realized that Hannah had made up her mind. With that, they decided to release her into my custody. I don't think the investigators cared much either way, to be honest.

Hannah and I headed home. The closer we got, the more uncomfortable she became. She practically hyperventilated as we pulled into the apartment complex's parking lot. The car barely came to a stop before Hannah jumped out of it and hurried into our apartment.

A few days passed. Hannah hadn't left the apartment; she just stayed in her room. I tried to talk to her about why she felt the need to run away, but every time I did, she just shut down. I thought maybe it was best to leave it alone and be done with it.

However, Scarlet and her vile family weren't done with us. They had given us an initial false sense of security when we didn't hear from or see them around the apartment complex since Hannah's return.

But one day, I heard scratching at the front door. I looked out the peephole and didn't see anything. Certain I heard a noise, I opened the door but kept the chain latched. I still didn't see anything. Curiosity overcame me, and I cautiously stepped outside.

There, leaning against the stucco wall, was a dead-looking voodoo doll with its mouth slashed. Scarlet and her family were sending Hannah a message.

That was it! I threw that demonic doll into the trash and got my Bible. I stormed my way over to Scarlet's apartment without any consideration for my own safety. I practically beat the door down like they owed me rent. Scarlet answered with her usual puffed-up attitude.

"What the hell do you want?" Scarlet smarted off.

Before I could respond, I looked into the living room behind Scarlet. It was nothing more than a hellish abyss. It was painted blood-red and saturated with perversion. It reeked of marijuana, cigarettes, stale sweat, and tainted sex. The furniture was worn down and stained with God only knows what, and the carpet was full of burn holes. The only light came from the illumination flickering off raunchy images in a music video playing on the television. But worst of all, I could feel the thick, ominous presence of the devil himself. The evil was so great that it made me take a few steps back.

After I steeled myself, I held my Bible up at Scarlet. It was my spiritual weapon because what was standing before me was no child. It was a demon in the flesh. God took over as I rebuked Scarlet with His Word. Scarlet cowered backward into the apartment as if my words were singeing her flesh. She slammed the door to block the Word of God from destroying her completely.

Satisfied, I went back home with the hope that everything would be okay. But just like money, hope was in short supply and finally lost when the truth was revealed about Solomon's friends—that they were really violent gang members. Solomon's crisis forced me to once again acknowledge the truth about my life, and I felt like giving up.

Good grief, I could never catch a break.

Chapter 24

Singing helped me during that particularly low point in my life. I made up songs that were more like prayers. They gave me the incentive to go forward, even though I couldn't see the purpose for my problems.

It was time to call my parents and update them on my life. I knew I'd face harsh criticism, so I sang to calm my nerves right before I spoke to them. After I told them what was happening with the children, they expressed concern about my inability to properly parent as a single mother. They pressured me to send my children to Africa to be raised by them only for a few months.

Though I was appreciative of the offer, the very thought of my children living in Africa caused me to shudder. I felt Solomon would rebel against my father's strict, patriarchal ways and that would cause a rift in the family. But I had to acknowledge that Solomon truly needed a male role model, and Daddy was a proper one.

Hannah, on the other hand, would face a different challenge in Africa. This was due to the fact that Hannah's motherly temperament was augmented by a strong will. Though I loved that aspect about her, the Congo didn't appreciate girls with fighting spirits. Life in the Congo would relentlessly tamp her down until she had no other choice but to wilt.

And then there was Walter. I had no idea where he was. If he was in Africa, he could lay claim to the children, and I'd never see them again.

All those scenarios were only possibilities. However, Hannah's involvement with Scarlet and Solomon's gang activity were real and immediate threats. I didn't know what to do and turned to an outside party for advice.

I told a traditional-thinking friend about my dilemma, thinking she'd side with my parents. Instead, my friend intuitively said, "You're right about Solomon. He might do okay. But it doesn't matter where Hannah goes. Her problem is not her location; it is a troubled spirit. That spirit will be with her wherever she goes. There's no escaping that."

My friend was right. Hannah's problems would be with her whether she was in Africa or America. This caused me to brood even more. After much prayer, I decided to send Hannah and Solomon to Africa. The two younger children needed to stay with me, especially Sophia, who was diagnosed with asthma.

The day came for me to see Hannah and Solomon off, and I felt an overwhelming sense of dread that I couldn't shake. As they boarded the plane, I tried to reassure myself that I was doing the right thing and that they'd be back soon. However, when I got into my car and saw the empty spots where Hannah and Solomon would've been sitting, I felt sick to my stomach.

Weeks passed. I was relieved that Walter did not appear to be in the Congo, but some of my other fears were coming true. Americanized Hannah was having difficulty conforming to the tribal culture. She was beginning to exhibit some unruly behavior that required my parents to constantly intervene to protect her from the cultural backlash.

I felt so guilty about what was happening to Hannah. It was because of my own failings that my children had to be sent away. This caused my self-esteem to plummet and my walk with Christ to be jeopardized because my faith was faltering.

Once again, I had to sing through my pain and worries. Little by little, my soul was liberated with each song I crooned. Later on, those same songs of faith buoyed me when I found out Hannah and Solomon wouldn't be allowed to return to America due to some technicalities regarding my own immigration case.

Their immigration cases would end up dragging on for years. The immigration suspected fraud on my part because, in their prejudiced opinion, who in her right mind would send her children from America *back* to Africa. Still, I kept fighting even when they later changed Hannah's immigration status to self-deported. That meant she would be ineligible to apply for a re-entry visa for ten years.

The longer Hannah stayed in the Congo, the more her life went down. Her teenage rebellion was in full swing, and my parents discovered that she'd fallen in with a bad crowd. I was terrified she'd end up just like me—that she'd be trapped by a slick man like Walter.

All I could do was pray that *something* would be put in Hannah's path to make her more responsible. God answered my prayer, but not in the way I expected. In 2006, Hannah called me to let me know she was pregnant. I wasn't surprised in the least bit, although it pained me to think about the hardship she was about to endure as a single mother. But I couldn't dwell on that. Hannah was scared and needed my support.

Nine months passed, and Joshua was born. Amazingly, that little bundle gave Hannah the desire to turn her life around. Hannah matured a great deal, trying her best to become a capable mother.

Hannah called me one day and told me about how she missed my singing. Now that she was a mother, she comforted Joshua with songs just like I'd done for her. She also told me I was a good mother.

Upon hearing those words, I put my hand on my chest as if Hannah's head was resting on it. I was so thankful she thought of me that way, even though my view of myself was the opposite. In spite of that, I closed our conversation with a song just for her.

Chapter 25

$\mathscr{L}$ ife went on, and only by the grace of God did I reach the year 2008. However, I was splintered in my mind, living a Jekyll and Hyde existence.

The Jekyll part of me was a realtor who was just coming into her own. Although I wasn't making big money, my business savvy and confidence were high. I had a decent car that allowed me to comfortably drive clients around. As they listened to my spiel, my charming sales smile would captivate them. Also, though I still had to buy work clothes on sale and at thrift stores, I was no longer relying on charitable donations. The money I was making kept the lights on in the cozy apartment I shared with Abigail and Sophia. I was proud that my girls were American—every bit of apple pie on the Fourth of July.

The Hyde side of me was more active and the holder of my depression and anxiety. The depression had me in a perpetual gloomy state despite my outward appearance. The accompanying anxiety made me wake up in full-blown panic attacks, hallucinating Walter's sinister presence in the darkness.

Whenever I looked in the mirror, all I saw was that same accusatory face staring back at me. It reminded me that I was still damaged, and if my two younger children were thriving, it was in spite of me. There were days when I could barely get out of bed. Other times, I wanted to jump into my car and just drive and keep driving with no destination in sight. I felt trapped, suffocated. I just wanted to get away from myself.

I was lost. Somewhere between Walter and my struggles to bring my children back home from Africa, my sanity started slipping away. It was true that God had been there so many times before to pick me up. However, I hadn't done the work to maintain His grace.

It came to me that I was worthless, and my family would've been better off without me. Thoughts of suicide filled my head and gave me a macabre sense of peace. I spent hours thinking about ways I could bring about my demise. Of course, I wanted it to be clean. I didn't want my parents to deal with any sort of gore. I thought about who would get what when I died and what kind of funeral I'd have.

But one day, I was watching my children play. They were so sweet and innocent. As they romped, their big eyes would land on me. Their eyes crinkled and sparkled with joy because they didn't see a depressed failure; they only saw their mother.

I knew right then that I had to spare my children the agony of losing their mother through the act of suicide. I needed help but couldn't go to the church. I had been perpetrating a fraud in the form of a praise-filled "Sister Celine" façade. I was a church leader who was expected to be nearly perfect, and I was not. I needed an impartial stranger to talk to, so I found a therapist who saw abused women for free and quickly started sessions.

The therapist was an instrument used by God to help me examine my behavior and life patterns. She helped me discover that the roots of my problems were unresolved issues with Daddy. Since childhood, I had longed for my father. I loved him so very much, but I didn't feel that he loved me back with the same intensity. I also had hidden anger stemming from Daddy's infidelity and outside children, who I saw as added competition for his affection.

As time went on, I made some progress with therapy, but the anxiety and depression still weren't budging. The therapist suggested that I take an antidepressant. The first pill I took made me yawn all day. Other side effects occurred, and I humbly asked God to take me to the next level of my therapy so that I could be rid of the demons of anxiety and depression without medication.

After that prayer, my next few counseling sessions were different. The therapist was able to recognize that I was holding back important information. She started asking more pointed questions, especially about Hannah. I was not at all pleased by the therapist's pushiness. I tried to shut down, but she didn't let me get away with avoiding her questions about Hannah. The more she probed, the more resistant I became.

The counseling sessions went on like that until one day the therapist decided to push me to the limits about Hannah. She kept at me until I broke down. In my teary confession, I revealed that Hannah reminded me too much of myself. Hannah just wanted to be loved by her father and acted out when that love was not forthcoming. It seared my soul to see Hannah go the same route I did, and I felt utterly helpless to stop it. When it came to Hannah, I thought I was the worst mother in the world because I didn't save her. Ultimately, if I couldn't save Hannah, I couldn't save me. I would never be more than an abused woman and a terrible mother, always struggling to survive. I was nothing … worse than nothing.

I could see a gentle smile appear on the therapist's face. She knew I had a breakthrough. With slender fingers, she pushed a bowl of colorful marbles toward me.

"Pick the one you like the best. The most precious looking one," the therapist said.

I picked one that looked like it had blue and purple mist swirling inside.

The therapist said, "From now on this is your marble to carry with you wherever you go. Whenever you look at it, picture yourself as this unique stone. Anytime you want to compromise your standards or believe you have no value, remember how precious and unique you are."

I clutched that marble and thought to myself, *I'm deserving of nothing but respect.* With feelings of tranquility and optimism, I rose from the chair.

That marble stayed with me for years. God used it to remind me, time and time again, that I was worth something. All the tribulations I endured had a purpose. Eventually, with that marble, I managed to achieve one victory after another and move toward healing.

Chapter 26

I had a dream once. In it, my brother was relocating, and his friend was there. This friend was also deeply in love with me. Though I could not make out the friend's face, he was oddly familiar. He kissed me with so much passion, and it seemed like it was really happening. The dream ended with the friend and me getting married.

Shortly after, I told my brother about the dream. His eyes widened with amazement. "The wife and I were contemplating moving to Canada and prayed to God for some confirmation that it would be a good move," he said.

As my brother relished in my premonition about his move, he ignored the other part of the dream ... the part about the friend. As he droned on, I wondered which one of my brother's friends would be my future lover. I went through the list of all the men my brother associated with. Most were married, too old, or simply not my type. No one was a viable candidate. But that didn't matter; I held on to the dream anyway.

The time came for my brother to relocate to Canada, and I was still very much single. The dream slowly faded into memory. I let go of any chance of being with my phantom lover. Instead, I gave most of my energy to Hannah and Solomon's immigration battle.

Despite this, the rest of my life was content. My real estate career was going well, and my two younger children were happy. Though I still suffered from low-level anxiety, it was controlled with meditation and hard workouts at the gym.

But I felt like my life had plateaued, and I was sometimes lonely for male companionship.

Life took a turn in 2009. The phone rang with an unfamiliar number on the Caller ID. I was used to getting those types of calls as a realtor and answered with a professional greeting.

"Hey, sis. This is Peter," said the soothing voice on the other end of the line.

My heart leapt. I hadn't seen Peter since Walter drove him from our home so many years earlier.

Peter and I went on to talk as though no time had passed. He gave me the rundown of his life, including the fact that he'd just gotten a divorce. When I heard that, I went from friend to counselor, assuming he called simply to vent. But it soon became evident that Peter had other intentions and was trying to feel me out.

That's when I cut the conversation short. I was afraid of Peter's romantic hints because of where I was in life. Though I was interested in dating, I was also fearful of complicating the stability and peace I had worked so hard for.

Peter sensed my trepidation and backed off. It took him one whole year to gather the courage to call me back, but when he did, he was determined to see me.

"I'll be in town for a conference, a screening of a documentary I'm involved in about street kids in the Congo. I'd very much like for you to come. Also, we *need* to talk," Peter said.

Peter's confidence convinced me to give in, and I agreed to meet him. However, I wondered what he needed to talk about.

The day of the conference finally arrived. I didn't consider my meeting with Peter to be a date, but I couldn't stop acting like it was. I got my hair done, made sure my makeup was perfect, and picked out a sexy yet sophisticated dress. I kept asking myself why I was acting like this was an official date.

Peter, after all, was just a childhood friend through my brother. However, the queasiness in my stomach told a different story.

When I arrived at the conference center, I was surrounded by posters featuring Peter's name and likeness. I picked up a brochure showcasing Peter's biography and an endless list of accomplishments. I couldn't help but be in awe of him.

I saw Peter as soon as I stepped into the main conference room. He was getting ready to go on stage but stopped as soon as he saw me. He hurried toward me with his arms widespread as usual.

"It's so nice to see you again, my sister," Peter said as he swallowed me in a hug. After Peter released me, he excitedly waved over his two children.

"Celine, I'd like you to meet Nina and Carl, my kids," Peter gushed. Peter's children hugged me like they'd known me their whole lives. Between them, I was the filling in a huge sandwich.

Peter was called to the stage and excused himself. Wide-eyed, I watched Peter walk confidently across the stage. But I was thrown off when the announcer introduced Peter as a father of two and *still* married. I was confused, but mostly jealous. That made no sense, to be jealous of Peter's now-broken marriage. However, as Peter spoke, my jealousy died down. I focused instead on his talent, intellect, and determination to actually make a film.

After the presentation, Peter pulled me aside and asked me not to leave. He still wanted to have that talk. As we made our way through the lobby with his children, a group of mutual acquaintances from Atlanta saw us. They expressed relief that Walter hadn't killed me and were delighted that I was doing well. However, as Peter and I walked away, I knew their gossipy tongues would start wagging. I didn't care.

Peter and I arrived at the pool. While the kids frolicked, we joked around. However, I could tell he wanted to say something more intimate, but the children's interruptions made that awkward. So, we just continued laughing and carrying on just like old times.

As the night drew to a close, Peter walked me to my car. Neither one of us wanted to say goodbye, so I invited him and the children over for a spaghetti dinner the next day. Peter immediately took me up on my invitation.

For a brief moment, my eyes locked on Peter's fixed gaze. As I stared at him staring at me, all sound around us silenced as if only the two of us existed. I could feel something awakening in me. It was exhilarating but scary. I knew that if I allowed myself to be vulnerable, I was risking being hurt again. On the other hand, this could've been the most beautiful experience of my life.

But my mind snapped back to reality and reminded me: *It's not that serious. It's just spaghetti.*

Chapter 27

After the conference, I couldn't stop wondering, *God, what are you up to?* I thought it best not to get too excited about Peter, but thoughts of him kept intruding into my mind. I went to bed wound up and restlessly tossed all night in anticipation of that spaghetti dinner.

Morning rolled in, and I got up feeling happy—happier than I'd been in a long time. I immediately proceeded to prepare the food, and there was plenty because Abigail and Sophia were away visiting relatives. Their absence eased some of the pressure because I would only have to manage myself.

When Peter and his children arrived, the inviting smell of pasta greeted them as they entered my spotless home. Even I looked immaculate on the outside, but on the inside, I was a wreck. I wanted so badly to make a good impression. Peter sensed this and took my hand.

"It's okay. Calm down. Everything is great. Your home. The food. *You.* It's all perfect," Peter said.

Peter's words relaxed my nervous heart, and then I was able to enjoy him and the scrumptious meal I'd prepared. Our conversation was lively, and I was all aglow as I watched Peter with his children. He was so tender and treated them with kindness and respect. The children, in turn, were light and carefree.

Though observing this enchanted me, I lamented about my own children. I wished they had been brought up by a father like Peter. If they had been, maybe Solomon would never have joined a gang, Abigail and Sophia would've had the affection of a doting father, and Hannah wouldn't have been abused like she was.

After dinner, Peter and I let the children go to the game room. This gave us a chance to continue our private talk. I could tell Peter had something he wanted to say, but he avoided being direct. Instead, he hinted at some unrequited feelings he had for me while we were growing up. He started talking about how he regretted his first marriage and thought I would've been a better wife. However, he said it in kind of a joking way, so I couldn't tell whether or not he was serious. Either way, I was comfortable with Peter. Being with him— whether as a friend or love interest—just felt right.

After our spaghetti dinner, Peter did get around to asking me out again. We met up at an open-air mall for some casual fun. As we walked around, the normally tacky background music was surprisingly romantic. It helped turn the ordinary mall into a Shangri-La and set the tone for the rest of the night.

We laughed as Peter told jokes, and I came back with a few of my own. Others smiled at us as if our laughter was a gift to their spirits. That is what joy does; it spreads to other people and causes them delight. But we were wrapped up in each other and basically oblivious to the crowd.

As we continued walking past storefronts, Peter's hand would occasionally brush against mine. His skin was like velvet, so soft to the touch. The warmth radiating from his hand sent tingles up my arm. I could tell he felt it, too. I'd catch him glancing over at me. He wasn't looking at me like I was a little sister; he was looking at me like I was a woman.

Night fell. The blackness of heaven was sprinkled with flickering, brilliant stars. It was as if the stars had been placed there just for us.

Peter and I came to a stream. He mischievously looked at me like he was challenging me to go in. I took my shoes off and stuck my feet right in. Peter did the same. We frolicked along the stream's edge, kicking up water like two children. I felt so good, almost like I was being baptized.

After a few minutes, Peter invited me to sit on a bench next to the stream. My heart was thumping because I knew that in a moment, we would never be the same again. Peter took my hand. He confessed his deep feelings for me, and I reciprocated. We decided to move forward with our relationship, now defined by new terms.

We stayed together until 4 a.m. It was time to say goodbye. As Peter walked me to my car, he suddenly stopped.

"May I please hug you?" Peter asked.

I was so impressed by Peter's chivalrous manner. He was definitely the polar opposite of Walter.

"Yes ... yes. I'd like that," I said.

I let myself go into Peter's arms. This hug was different from all the ones he'd given me before. As my body pressed into his, I knew the gravity of this hug. Now we were adults involved in a romance. This was our first hug as lovers.

Both of our hearts were beating hard and fast. As our embrace tightened, I made sure to savor the moment. I took note of the woodsy-ness of his cologne, the bulge of his muscles, and the heat of his breath lingering around my neck. We stayed in each other's arms as long as we could. That was one of the longest goodbyes I ever had.

That simple date heralded a transformative period in my life. My relationship with Peter, once sibling-like, did blossom into a wonderful courtship. He made me feel things that I thought were dead in me like relief, peace, and ease. As my libido reawakened, I was no longer afraid to feel. I was alive.

However, Abigail and Sophia weren't so open to Peter. They had been with me throughout the years and experienced the financial and mental health struggles I'd dealt with. They had seen me sad so many times and put me in their little protective cocoon. They were also aware of the predators who were waiting to take advantage of a some-times naïve woman such as me and were determined that no one would hurt me again.

The girls were also wrestling with their trust issues revolving around Walter.

Sophia had vague, infantile memories of Walter. Random images of that barbarian would sometimes flicker through her mind's eye. Some images were just of him roaming through our home like some large animal. Other fleeting images were more frightening. She could see Walter's lips curled back in anger. Sometimes she saw his hazy fists pounding the table if the food wasn't right. She could even slightly remember seeing my blood drops on the floor. This left her skeptical of any man's intentions toward her or me. Naturally, she didn't believe in romance and had little faith that a man could truly love a woman.

Abigail's memories weren't nebulous like Sophia's. Her memories were spectacularly vivid and fiery. Walter's rage and violence were indelibly etched in her memory like a scar.

Whenever Abigail was triggered to remember, she wanted to lash out at Walter. But he wasn't there, so she had to decide whether to push her rage down or deal with it. She knew if she tried to put the rage away, she'd end up like Hannah, struggling to process the past.

Abigail decided that her rage wouldn't handicap her. She used it as a motivating force, especially when it came to sports. She gathered all her hatred of Walter and channeled it into running. She eventually became a star on her high school track team. While other students looped around the track with thoughts of scholarships or adoration pushing them toward the finish line, Abigail was inspired by Walter.

With swift feet, Abigail imagined Walter chasing her. The closer he got, the faster she ran. With Walter at her back, Abigail broke some records.

At least Walter was good for something.

Chapter 28

$\mathscr{A}$ bigail and Sophia put up a mighty front against Peter, but he took their coldness and suspicion in stride. He knew the girls were hurt and felt only compassion for their plight.

However, Peter was on his own mission. He was in love with me and had committed to a vision of his future. That future not only included me, but also all of our children. He wouldn't be diverted from his plan, so the more Abigail and Sophia resisted him, the more his love for them grew.

Little by little, the purity of Peter's intentions wore down the girls' defenses. Their hearts reluctantly started to soften. Eventually, they let go of their mistrust and surrendered to love. It seemed as if a burden had been lifted off them. See, they had actually liked Peter from the start, but fear masked it. Now the burdensome fear was gone, and the girls could have the father they always wanted and deserved.

Peter was more than thrilled to take over the part of a father. He became the girls' advisor and comforter just like their heavenly Father. He ran errands with them and attended all of their extracurricular activities. He also gave them an extra brother and sister through Nina and Carl. Abigail and Sophia even started calling him Papa P.

Once that hurdle was passed, Peter knew it was time to formally make us a family. Although I knew Peter loved me deeply, I was still surprised when he proposed to me. He was barely done asking before I enthusiastically said, "Yes!"

Peter and I got married in September 2010. As I stood facing him at the altar, I was awestruck by how incredible he was.

He looked so much like an angel as he looked lovingly into my eyes.

As the pastor officiated, I said a silent prayer praising God. I was so thankful that God put this precious man in my life—the actual husband my heavenly Father prepared for me since the beginning of time.

In return, I promised God I'd be a comfort for Peter as well. As I recited my formal vows, I thought about Proverbs 18:22. I would be that good wife, no matter what. Peter, the good man, deserved to finally have that. The breakup of his first marriage was devastating to him, and he suffered through it silently and alone. I was determined to erase his pain, feelings of rejection, and sense of betrayal. After all, he'd done that for me. I would let God work through me to restore him and be his second chance. Consequently, our God-ordained love would allow us to individually reach our full potentials, and together we'd be an example for other God-fearing couples to follow.

Other things in my life were going well, too. The immigration officials finally allowed Solomon to come home. I was overjoyed but fretted over how Solomon and Peter would get along. However, my fears were assuaged when the two finally met.

Solomon was no longer the rebellious boy who left me; he was now a responsible young man who only wanted me to be happy. Solomon also saw that Peter was a fine and noble man who not only took care of me but also loved and cared for our family.

The next year, I got another wonderful gift. Hannah was allowed to return to the United States. Unfortunately, the immigration officials wouldn't let Joshua come with her. Regardless, I was still thrilled to see Hannah. She had changed so much over the years. She was now a woman with a child of her own, and she had matured a lot. However, some things had stayed the same.

Hannah's old soul was still struggling to be in this world. She had not had therapy or anyone to talk to about her personal problems while she was in the Congo. All the pain she'd gone through was still fresh. On top of that, she felt like she'd let me down by becoming a single mother.

The first few days Hannah was home, she languished a bit, though she was glad to see us. She not only had to readjust to American culture but also longed for Joshua. However, being away from Joshua stoked her guilt and caused her to distance herself from him, for fear of being a failure as a mother.

My reaction toward Hannah's behavior wasn't compassion; it was an irritation. I couldn't understand why she seemed to be purposefully sabotaging herself. After all, she witnessed the mayhem I went through and should've learned from it. I was determined to confront her instead of sidestepping as I'd done before.

At first, my intention was to be lovingly tough. I said, "I know you think you're the only one who has made mistakes. But you've been with me through the years, and you know I've made more mistakes than most. If you continue on this path, it will not only destroy you, but also Joshua."

Hannah looked up at me with embarrassment in her eyes. At that moment, I had an epiphany. It came over me as if I had been struck by lightning. I finally realized that I wasn't there to save Hannah; Hannah was sent by God to save me. As the sacrificial lamb, Hannah had been carrying burdens for the rest of the family.

I thought about the trappings of my new life: a superb husband, great career, and all my children under one roof. They were the products of catalysts brought about by Hannah. I couldn't give my blameful speech anymore. Instead, I took Hannah in my arms and gave her thanks.

At that moment, I resolved to use Hannah's experiences as examples of strength and love to help other young women like her.

Chapter 29

I reached a point where it appeared I had everything I wanted, but there was still something I longed to have. I desperately wanted total freedom from the psychic shackles Walter had on me.

Walter's monstrous image continued to terrorize my dreams. I'd wake up sometimes shaking and damp with sweat. Daylight hours were no better. If I was alone, I thought I'd catch glimpses of him out of the corner of my eye. I could still hear the echo of his screaming voice in my ears.

I thought about going back on antidepressants. I knew that wouldn't solve my problem, but I needed to sleep at night and function during the day. Also, I was trying to avoid reverting back to the nervous wreck I'd been years earlier.

Peter was the only thing that stood between me and the drugs. He was my solace. Whenever I was feeling overwhelmed and anxious, I could rely on Peter. I always felt better after leaning on his shoulder or getting a hug from him. His sweet kisses and hugs were salves for my soul. Those lovely, innocent moments spent with him were infused with freshness and hopeful anticipation of good things. When Peter was around, elusive joy came back. Truthfully, his presence alone helped me to stay sane.

But Peter always had to leave. He was commuting back and forth between Raleigh, where he worked as a scientist, and Dallas. Whenever he left, those doldrums came back, along with the nightmares. I got to the point where I was afraid to go to sleep when Peter was away.

Those long separations were difficult but made our reunions even more glorious. However, Peter became weary of commuting after a year of flying between the two cities and decided to permanently join me. Needless to say, I was thrilled at the prospect of having Peter home on a full-time basis. I thought that maybe Walter's ghost would finally disappear once Peter came home.

I started making arrangements for the move ASAP. In fact, I may have gotten overzealous with the preparations at times. It's just that I really wanted Peter at home because I missed him terribly.

I flew to Raleigh and we opted for the long road drive to Dallas. Planning the road trip was exciting because I knew that would be the last time we'd have to commute.

When I made it to Raleigh, I didn't even want to play the tourist. I just wanted to get Peter packed and moved. Peter donated all his furniture and appliances to a young family who had just immigrated into the United States. He then ground shipped some other boxes and equipment to Dallas. As we loaded the remaining boxes and suitcases in the car, I felt so much happiness as yet another chapter in my life was beginning. Nothing would stop the goodness God had prepared for me, not this time. I just knew it.

But as Peter and I were driving back to Dallas, he decided the best route would be through Atlanta. Suddenly, all the air was sucked out of the car. It seemed as though the past was barreling down on me.

"No, why don't we just cut through another town. I'm sure it would be shorter," I said, trying not to sound panicked.

Peter replied, "I think it would be good not only to go through Atlanta, but back to your old apartment. I see how you toss at night, dreaming, and sometimes you seem to be so sad. I think you need to clear."

I had no idea Peter could tell I was having nightmares about Walter. I thought I'd kept that a guarded secret. But I played dumb. "Clear? What do you mean?"

"Clear the memory of Walter out of you, so you can be at peace."

As much as I wanted to resist, I knew Peter was right. The ghost of Walter was haunting me and would never let me go. I had to release myself. I lowered my head as if I was preparing to go to a funeral.

I said, "Okay, let's do it." Peter rerouted the GPS and we went off to Atlanta, and that hellhole of an apartment.

Peter held my hand as he drove us back to the apartment complex I used to live in. I kept looking at the car's side mirror and searching for any sign of Walter. The faces in the other cars all seemed to look like his. I held my stomach as nausea set in.

When we got to the apartment complex, I almost didn't recognize it. It looked so rundown and desolate, more than it did when I lived there. It looked so bad that I wondered if it was even possible for people to still be there. As the car rolled over giant potholes, I saw men aimlessly hanging out on curbs and unsupervised children running around. Obnoxious music was blaring out of apartments, on sidewalks, and from junk cars.

This is where people go to die, I thought.

The car continued to make its way to my old apartment. I started having trouble catching my breath and began coughing. Tears welled up in my eyes as awful memories reminded me why I never wanted to go back to that horrible place.

"Are you alright? You look sick," Peter said, trying to drive and look at me at the same time.

I coughed like I was choking. "Just keep going before I change my mind."

Then I saw it: the old apartment. Vomit hit the back of my throat. I wanted to jump out of the car and run away, but Peter turned to me, his eyes filled with compassion.

"You can do this. You have to do this," Peter said. He was right again. I had to go there. I had to heal. I had to rid myself of the evil plaguing me.

Peter helped me out of the car because I was feeling weak and lightheaded. As I walked toward the apartment, I remembered how I dreaded seeing Walter in the window. But this time, I walked with a protective husband who loved me. With Peter by my side, I straightened up and walked tall.

Every step took me further into the past, and much to my surprise, I was able to find some goodness. The same trees were there and looked as if their leaves were unfurling with gladness to see me. I looked at my old balcony and saw faint images of my children gleefully playing on it. My eyes gazed upon the doors of former neighbors who did more than just take care of me when Walter was out of control; they were also my good friends.

I looked at Peter and nodded with understanding. He took me into his arms as I wept. Those tears were not the result of despair. They were tears of healing. We had done all we needed to do.

We got back into the car and proceeded to leave Atlanta. As we merged onto the interstate, I thought back on my quest to find my Prince Charming. I had indeed found him—but he wasn't Peter.

I knew, considering all that I'd gone through, that my real Prince Charming was God. He'd been there all along. Peter was just one of the many gifts my royal "King" had bestowed upon me.

As the city faded out behind us, I knowingly smiled a little. I was resurrected and able to walk fully with my ultimate bridegroom, God.

I was finally loosed.

Chapter 30

My life is a letter inspired by Christ to the entire world. As hard as it may be to believe, I think it was good that I was afflicted. Those valleys and mountains made me who I am. There is nothing I would choose to take out or do differently.

I'm enlightened enough to know that we all go through seasons. We may fight the inevitable destiny God has put before us by crafting our own human image, but only God knows what's behind the façade. He knows that real success is not the acquisition of material wealth or professional accolades; it is in the performance of service to others. I reckon that is why I had to go through my own suffering: so I could help others come through like me.

There was a time when I looked back on the painful events of my life and asked God how they could be put to positive use. It didn't take long for Him to answer. He worked through my pastor. The pastor mentioned that a lady came to her complaining about her abusive husband. The husband had tried to strangle her. My mind immediately flashed back to when Walter was strangling me. I could actually feel Walter's invisible hands crushing my neck.

As I scratched at my neck, I listened to the pastor's bizarre and naïve solution. She told the young woman to ask her father what to do. Fortunately, the father was an intelligent man and told the young lady to leave.

However, in many of our community churches and families, women in domestic violence situations are simply told to either pray the abuse away or hide what's going on—basically, to protect the image of the abuser. The backgrounds of ministers and the cultures of the women may deem certain atrocities as acceptable in order to keep communal peace and uphold traditions.

I was disturbed by the way women were seen as disposable and was determined to do something about it. I started counseling battered women in a way radically different from the church's way. Instead of telling them to pray or keep their mistreatment quiet, I told them to find the courage to leave. It helped quite a few women, but I felt I could reach many more who were trapped in abusive relationships.

Then it dawned on me that I could write a book.

The work was arduous and painful and took many years. This book is my tribute to God for all the good He gave me. Every day, my heart grows light with the knowledge that the book's God-inspired words can frighten and enlighten someone enough to leave an abusive situation before it's too late.

Though parts of my life were painful, degrading, and terrifying, they served a purpose and mattered. I can now use my experience to help in a way that others cannot. I am merely the first link in a long chain that will be added to as another battered woman is saved, and then another, and then another.

Thank you so much for being part of my journey. My wish is for you to be stronger and better for the next one.